T0353723

BASICS FOR BIBLE INTERPRETATION

Copyright 2017 Lawrence Chipao

Luviri Press
P/Bag 201
Luwinga, Mzuzu 2
Malawi

ISBN 978-99960-968-9-1

eISBN 978-99960-60-21-2

Luviri Press wird außerhalb Malawis vertreten durch:

African Books Collective Oxford (orders@africanbookscollective.com)

www.africanbookscollective.com

Cover: Josephine Kawejere

BASICS FOR BIBLE INTERPRETATION

Biblical Hermeneutics

LAWRENCE CHIPAO

LUVIRI PRESS

MZUZU

2017

CONTENTS

GLOSSARY OF TERMS

Biblical hermeneutics. The science and art of interpreting God's word and making sound applications.

Biblical theology. The study of the progressive revelation of divine truth throughout the Old Testament and New Testament.

Culture. The common ideas, beliefs, and customs shared and accepted by people in a society (Summers, 2001, 330).

Homiletics. The science and art of effectively communicating the Word of God to others through preaching. As it relates to the content of the text, the preacher's task is to accurately communicate biblical truth to his or her hearers.

Illumination. The act of God the Holy Spirit guiding the Spirit-indwelt reader into the truth of Scripture and leading the reader to an extra-exegetical understanding of the general truth of God's Word. (Note: The term "extra-exegetical" is not meant to imply that the Holy Spirit is not involved in the process of exegesis, but that illumination is properly understood to be an aspect of the convicting role of the Spirit to soften and prepare one's heart to receive God's Word. God speaks to us through His written Word, and the Spirit helps us to know that what we are reading is indeed God's Word).

Inspiration. The act of God the Holy Spirit superintending the writing of Scripture. (Note: The term "superintending" is used to acknowledge that God uses the personality, experience, vocabulary, and writing style of the biblical author in producing Scripture. Inspiration is divine guidance, not dictation. By superintending the biblical authors, God ensured that His revelation to mankind was recorded accurately and without error).

Interpretation. The prayerful application of Scriptural principles by which the illuminated student of God's Word comes to an understanding of Scripture that corresponds as closely as humanly possible to the inspired meaning. The Holy Spirit reveals general truths about God; the student, convicted of these general truths, applies hermeneutic principles to arrive at its proper meaning.

Revelation. The act of God the Holy Spirit unveiling truth to man.

Systematic Theology. The study that organizes biblical data into logical rather than historical categories. The systematic theologian attempts to gather all of the biblical data together on a given topic (e.g., Christology, Pneumatology) in order to deduce the totality of God's revelation on the topic. (Virkler 1981, 18)

INTRODUCTION

In this simple-to-read book I am presenting some basics for Bible interpretation. My main purpose is to ensure that any serious reader of the Bible is able to grasp each biblical authors' intended meaning in writing their particular portion of Scripture. I also want the reader to be able to apply the truths learned to every applicable context of life. I truly believe that anyone can interpret the Bible, and that he or she can do so without distorting its meaning—so long as they follow the right interpretative principles.

I have therefore attempted to present these basic principles in the simplest manner possible. At the same time, I have sought to present every principle one might need to properly interpret Scripture and make sound applications. My word to you, dear reader, is that, prayerfully, you take time with this book. What you will learn in its pages will surely take you to the desired destination, and it will do so without causing weariness or boredom. I am sure that you will be rewarded a hundred-fold for your effort.

My sincere ambition is to see committed ministers of the Gospel and Christians who will commit themselves to finish the feasible task of taking the Gospel to the ends of the earth before the soon coming of Christ (Matthew 24:14). Surely, we must appreciate the supremacy of the Holy Spirit in this great task.

CHAPTER 1

DEFINING BIBLICAL INTERPRETATION THEMES

A clear understanding of hermeneutical key terms is essential to understanding the process of biblical interpretation. In this chapter, we will zero in on defining some key terms to be used in the study.

Biblical Interpretation

Biblical interpretation is the systematic application of the principles used to reveal the true meaning of Scripture. The purpose of the discipline is that the interpreter may know God more intimately and serve Him more perfectly. Douglas P. Lowenberg defines biblical interpretation as "a study of principles that guide one to expose the inspired meaning embodied in the text of Scripture." He further explains, "The first step, exegesis, seeks to find the original meaning of the text; the second step, hermeneutics, expresses the meaning in today's context (Lowenberg 2006, 12).

Hermeneutics

Hermeneutics is both a science and an art. It is a science in that it teaches the principles and methods of interpreting God's Word. It is an art in that it guides the interpreter in making sound applications of those principles based on certain interpretative rules. Milton S. Terry says,

> Hermeneutics, therefore, is both a science and an art. As a science, it enunciates principles, investigates the laws of thought and language, and classifies its facts and

results. As an art, it teaches what application these principles should have, and establishes their soundness by showing their practical value in the elucidation of the more difficult scriptures. The hermeneutical art thus cultivates and establishes a valid exegetical procedure (Terry 1978, 20).

In much the same way, Bernard Ramm writes "Hermeneutics is the science and art of Biblical interpretation. It is a science because it is guided by rules within a system; and it is an art because the application of these rules is by skill and not by mechanical imitation" (Ramm 1995, 1).

Exegesis

Exegesis involves the application of hermeneutical principles and laws aimed at discovering the original, intended meaning of the author. The word *exegesis* is formed by combining two Greek words *ex*, meaning out of, and *egeisthas*, meaning to lead or guide. To exegete, then, is "to lead out of." Walter C. Kaiser, Jr., distinguishes hermeneutics from exegesis:

> Therefore, while hermeneutics will seek to describe the general and special principles and rules which are useful in approaching the Biblical text, exegesis will seek to identify the single truth-intention of individual phrases, clauses, and sentences as they make up the thought of paragraphs, sections, and, ultimately, entire books. Accordingly, hermeneutics may be regarded as the *theory* that guides exegesis; exegesis may be understood in this work to be the *practice* of and the set of the *procedures* for discovering the author's intended meaning (Kaiser 1994, 47).

Similarly, Henry A. Virkler defines exegesis as an "application of the principles of hermeneutics to understand the author's intended meaning." He distinguishes biblical theology from systematic theology stating that "biblical theology organizes those meanings in a historical manner while systematic theology arranges those meanings in a logical fashion" (Virkler 1981, 45). Terry notes that practically "exegesis is related to hermeneutics as preaching is to homiletics" (Terry 1978, 19).

Eisegesis

Unfortunately, people often attempt to interpret Scripture by using what is known as *eisegesis*, rather than exegesis. As just stated, exegesis occurs when one objectively draws the meaning *from* the text. On the other hand, eisegesis occurs when one subjectively reads meaning *into* the text. In doing this, one conceives a meaning for the text in their mind without following the rules of good hermeneutics, and then he or she reads that preconceived meaning into the text. The Bible reader must take caution against doing eisegesis; it is the wrong approach in handling the Word of God.

The Interpreter

Before attempting to interpret Scripture, it is important that the interpreter first understands himself or herself. This is because the way a person sees himself affects the way he interprets the Word. One's faith in God inevitability determines how much he or she will believe that the Bible is God's inspired and authoritative Word. Similarly, the way one views the Bible will dramatically determine the level of his or her faith in God.

Further, one's identity as a Christian has an impact on how he or she approaches the Bible. If one is not a Christian, it will be difficult for him to understand many of the concepts and terms used in Scripture. For instance, he or she will struggle to embrace and identify with the supernatural experiences spoken of in Scripture. In such a situation, one may read the Bible as the Ethiopian Eunuch mentioned in the book of Acts. What he read from the book of Isaiah made no sense until Peter interpreted it for him (Acts 8:30-35).

Additionally, one's experience with the Holy Spirit will affect the way he or she approaches Scripture. The fact that the Bible was given through the inspiration of the Holy Spirit cannot be minimized (2 Peter 1:21). Therefore, the person who is full of the Holy Spirit is better prepared to interpret the Bible (1 Corinthians 2:14). Believing that one can fully understand Scripture without the presence of the Holy Spirit illuminating it is a fallacy. Jesus declared, "That which is born of the flesh is flesh, and that which is born of the Spirit is spirit" (John 3:6). Spiritual birth and Holy Spirit baptism are basic to interpreting Scripture. Any ordinary human being who has not been "born of the Spirit" is only "born of the flesh" and cannot understand spiritual matters in any way. Paul averred, "The natural person does not accept the things of the Spirit of God, for they are folly to him, and he is not able to understand them because they are spiritually discerned (1 Cor. 2:14). In summary, the interpreter must be born again, have faith in God, be filled with the Spirit, and be willing to obey the Word. Additionally, he or she should humbly depend on the Holy Spirit for guidance.

CHAPTER 2

BASIC PRINCIPLES OF BIBLICAL INTERPRETATION

Basic Truths

The Bible interpreter needs to have some basic understandings about the Word of God. For instance, he or she needs to understand that the Bible was co-authored by God and certain divinely chosen men of God. He or she further needs to understand that the Bible is eternal, and, if properly interpreted, it can be understood by people of all times and in every cultural setting. This truth is foundational to sound biblical interpretation.

It is also important to understand that each biblical author wrote to a specific group of people in a specific historical-geographical setting for a specific purpose. He wrote in the language of the target audience using the local grammatical rules and figures of speech common to those people as well as to the writer himself. Then, the target people group read or understood what was written in the light of their unique cultural contexts.

However, since the Bible was also authored by God, it speaks of spiritual issues that can only be understood with the help of the Holy Spirit. Although it has many human authors, because the Bible was inspired by the Holy Spirit, it exhibits a cohesive unity throughout and never contradicts itself. Further, it has a clear progression from the beginning of creation in Genesis to the culmination of history in Revelation.

Challenges in Interpreting the Bible

It is important to note that the 66 books of the Bible were written by about 40 authors over a time span of about 1,500 years from about 3,500 to 2,000 years ago. As a result, modern readers of Scripture face several interpretative challenges if they are to understand what the authors meant to say and how they were understood by their original audiences. This challenge is especially true in African contexts where there is an unhealthy tendency to wrongly allegorize and spiritualize the Bible. In line with the fact that many are not aware of the sound principles of interpretation needed to properly understand Scripture, African church leaders, Bible school teachers, and church members struggle to interpret the Bible. In addition, many interpreters are simply careless in their approach to interpreting this Word of Truth.

I have personally observed a pattern among African preachers who listen to media preachers perceived to be the authorities in the Word. In so doing, they uncritically accept what such preachers teach, and then preach those same so called "truths" to their congregations. Sadly, many African sermons are jam-packed with radio, television, and internet media messages that, in most cases, have not been critically analyzed as to whether or not they have been derived from sound hermeneutics. Unfortunately, I know of no book aimed at helping African interpreters understanding the basic principles of sound biblical interpretation. Most books I have read on the subject fail to discuss the basic issues the elementary interpreter needs to understand to be an excellent student of the Bible.

In this same line of thinking, other issues that demand consideration, such as,

- whether or not God intended to convey a "fuller meaning" to Scripture than what the human author understood when he wrote,
- how to determine when a passage is to be interpreted literary, figuratively, or symbolically, and
- how one's personal commitment to God and His mission affects his or her ability to understand spiritual truth (Virkler 1981, 46).

As I have stated, there are several challenges Bible interpreters encounter in relation to the way the Bible was written. These include time gap, cultural gap, geographical distance, language gap, philosophical gap and covenant gap. Let's now talk about those issues.

Time Gap

It is important to read the Bible with the understanding that there exists a major time gap between the time the various books of the Bible were written and when we read it. Some of the materials in the Bible were written as early as 1440 BC. It should be obvious that the way people thought in those days was significantly different from the way we think today. Similarly, in some instances there was a significant time gap between when certain biblical authors wrote and when the events they describe took place. For example, the stories of Genesis happened long before Moses wrote about them. He was able to accurately recount these stories through the inspiration of the Holy Spirit. Other biblical historians faced similar challenges.

Cultural Gap

Here in Malawi, there are several people groups, each with their own culture. As a result, I sometimes find it difficult to understand why my friends from other cultures do certain things the way they do them—even though we live in the same small country. From 2001 to 2004, I was privileged to serve as a missionary in the country of Zimbabwe, one of Malawi's neighbouring countries. While there, I was bewildered by some of their cultural practices. They were so strange to me and my family.

We often face this same dilemma when reading the stories in the Bible. Biblical authors wrote to, and about, people who had their own customs, traditions, beliefs and practices. These customs may or may not have similarities to ours. Therefore, when interpreting their stories, we must keep in mind that many of their customs and practices were very different from ours, and therefore, at times they can be very difficult for us to understand.

It is also very difficult to know which areas are similar to, or different from, our own culture. For example, during worship in the Jewish synagogues the women were not allowed to sit in the same room with men. Therefore, their meeting places included a partition wall separating the men from the women. This practice seems strange to people from my culture; however, to Muslims in my country, who adopted this practice from the Arabic culture, it may seem normal.

For instance, consider this story from the Old Testament book of Ruth (3:1-14). Reflect on the scandal that would have

16

resulted in an African village if one evening a young lady would have crept into a man's house and slept by his bedside because she wanted to be married to him. In most African contexts, no man would want to marry such a woman. She would be considered a prostitute. She would become the talk of the village. However, this was an acceptable practice in the early Hebrew culture. It was the practice of a kinsman, or relative-redeemer, and there was no scandal involved.

Geographical Distance

Even in these modern days of mass communication, it is still difficult for people living in one part of a country to know what is happening in another area of the same country. I remember that in the 1970s, for one to travel from Blantyre to Lilongwe, a journey of about 350 km, took about fifteen hours by public transport. Today, it takes only four to five hours. In Bible times travel was much more difficult, and it took much longer to get from one place to another. Therefore, what seems like a short distance to us today would seem to them to be a very long and laborious journey.

Most of us live very far from the lands of the Bible, and most of us will never be able to visit such places. As a result, when we read in the Gospel of John that Jesus "had to go through Samaria" (John 4:4), it has little significance to us. We wonder, why would John even mention that Jesus had to go through Samaria? But, when we better understand the geographical setting of the Holy Land, and the strained relationships between the Jews and the Samarians, we would well understand what such a shortcut journey meant.

Language Gap

The Old Testament was mainly written in Hebrew, and the New Testament was written in the Greek language. Jesus spoke in the local language of Aramaic. None of these languages are in common usage today. Further, the Hebrew of the Old Testament is different from the Hebrew spoken in Israel today. The Greek of the New Testament is considered a dead language today, since it is no longer in use. Although biblical scholars struggle to learn these biblical languages, today no one uses them in dialogue. They are learned only to be able to better grasp what the biblical writers meant when they wrote to people in their time and in their cultures.

Further, no one today is able to completely understand the Greek of the New Testament, and therefore, they are unable to translate it without difficulty. Some biblical translators attempt to translate the text literally, while others translate merely according to their "mother language translation." What I mean by the phrase, *mother language translation,* is that a translation into a Western language may differ significantly from a translation into an African or Far Eastern language. This, however, should not discourage anyone seeking to interpret the Bible, but should encourage them to learn good hermeneutical principles. One does not need to speak Greek or Hebrew to properly interpret the Bible; however, one does need to follow sound principles of biblical interpretation. This being said, learning the biblical languages can, indeed, help one to understand the Bible, and if you ever get a chance to study one or all of these languages, do so. There are dividends from this.

The Philosophical Gap

The philosophical gap between the modern reader of Scripture and its original readers has to do with how each one views life. Each culture has its own worldview. That is, each culture has its own unique ideas about the nature and meaning of the universe that differ from other cultures. As a result, some worldviews may be similar to our own, while others may be very different. In a similar manner, it may be difficult for one to grasp the worldviews of the original biblical writers because of this philosophical gap between cultures. These philosophical differences are often expressed by using unique cultural expressions known as idioms. This too, presents a challenge for the contemporary Bible interpreter.

Covenant Gap

Finally, a "covenant gap" exists between today's Bible readers and the Old Testament biblical writers. A covenant is a formal agreement between two or more parties. Edwin Hartill defines a biblical covenant as "an agreement or a contract between men or between men and God (Hartill 1973, 19). Another term used for covenant is *testament*. This is where we get the idea of an Old Testament (or covenant) and a New Testament (or covenant). In the Bible, God made eight covenants with mankind. The first seven covenants are contained in the Old Testament, the final one appears in New Testament. All of these covenants reflect God progressive fulfillment of His mission to redeem fallen mankind.

The seven Old Testament covenants differ from the New Covenant in many ways; however, it is important to understand that all the covenants of the Old Testament lead us to the New Covenant. The New Testament is the fulfillment of the Old Testament. Nevertheless, the fact that we live under the New Covenant rather than the Old Covenant has many implications to both Christian and non-Christian, today.

CHAPTER 3

THE IMPORTANCE OF BIBLICAL INTERPRETATION

For any serious follower of Christ, sound biblical interpretation is not an option. In this chapter, we will seek to understand why it is so important that we learn to apply the principles of biblical interpretation to our study of the Bible. We will find it to be a rewarding exercise.

Once we understand the importance of truly knowing what the Bible teaches, we will be encouraged to take the required time to learn the principles of biblical interpretation. As a result, our churches will begin to move away from regularly promoting false doctrine to proclaiming the true teachings of Scripture. In like manner, in our biblical discussions, whether in home groups or Sunday school classes, we will begin to appreciate the teachings of Scripture using sound interpretative principles.

The prophet declared, "My people are destroyed from lack of knowledge" (Hosea 4:6). This should never be the case in our churches. Christians should not be allowed to perish because they have not been given the tools needed to dig out the true message of the Word of God. If they are not given such tools, they will inevitably make improper applications of Scripture. On the other hand, those who learn to apply the principles of sound biblical interpretation will be blessed in several important ways.

Understanding the Context

First, those who have learned to properly interpret Scripture will understand that the Bible was written by 40 divinely-

21

inspired authors over a period of about 1500 years. Such an insight alone will positively influence how they approach the Word of God. They will begin to see how the Bible had meaning to those people who first read its words, and in the same way, how it has meaning to Christians living today. Understanding such truths will help Christians to understand the right meanings of Scripture, and therefore, it will help them to make right applications for their lives.

Hermeneutics and True Worship

Next, a proper understanding of Scripture will help to lead people into true worship of the God who inspired Scripture. It will help Christians in their worship in at least two significant ways:

Discovering true worship

True worship comes from a clear understanding of who God is (John 4:24), and this understanding comes from a true understanding of the Word of God (2 Timothy 2:15). Further, this understanding of the Word of God can come only from sound biblical interpretation. Therefore, those who preach and teach the Word of God must have the skills necessary to properly interpret Scripture and to teach their people about the true God and how to truly worship Him (Hebrews 11:6).

Formulating biblical liturgy

Liturgy speaks of how Christians conduct their worship services. Every Christian church has its own particular liturgy. It is important that these liturgies be Bible-based. Therefore, in order for them to reflect what the Bible says, sound principles of biblical interpretation must be applied.

Hermeneutics and Authentic Ministry

Jesus commanded us to "go and make disciples of all nations" (Matthew 28:19). We have further been called to be "competent ministers of a new covenant" (2 Corinthians 3:6). In other words, we are called to be authentic ministers of the Gospel. We can do these things only if we clearly understand and teach the true meaning of Scripture. A proper understanding of the principles of biblical interpretation will help us do this in at least three important ways:

Effective preaching and teaching

Nowhere does the need for correct biblical interpretation come to the foreground more than in the areas of preaching and teaching the Word of God. These foundational ministries will produce their divinely-intended results only when ministers use sound biblical interpretation. Correct biblical interpretation reveals the true meaning of Scripture preparing the way for powerful application in the lives of believers. As a result, saints are caused to "grow in the grace and knowledge of our Lord and Saviour Jesus Christ" (2 Peter 3:18).

Effective pastoral care

Everyone needs pastoral care. This includes both lay people and ministers of the Gospel. Such ministry is essential for every Christian's spiritual growth and survival. Good pastoral care thus helps Christians and ministers to live lives "worthy of the Gospel of Christ" (Philippians 1:27). This ministry, however, will produce maximum positive results only if it is based squarely on a correct handling of the Word of God. This calls for correct biblical interpretation that will, in turn, produce sound biblical application.

Facilitating spiritual formation

While spiritual formation involves reading and understanding the Word, it is more than that. "It is a process concerned with holistic growth and development of the individual" (Anthony 2005, 91). Once a person is saved, the process of spiritual formation should continue the rest of their lives. Proper interpretation of Scripture will help these Christians to know God better and to understand how to make Him known to others. This entire process demands the correct handling of the Word of God.

Enjoying God

The Westminster Catechism teaches, "Man's chief end is to glorify God and to enjoy Him forever." However, a proper understanding of the Word of God is necessary for a Christian to do these things. It is true, believers are the happiest people in the world. However, this truth can never be fully appreciated in the lives of Christians until they clearly understand what the Bible teaches about them and "what God has prepared for those who love him" (1 Corinthians 2:9). This understanding will come only when believers study the Word and understand its teachings.

This knowledge must be based on the principles of sound biblical interpretation. It is, therefore, essential for every

Christian to develop these interpretative skills both for their own sake and for the sake of the Kingdom of God. When it comes to understanding the principles of biblical interpretation, there is no option for Christians and ministers of the Gospel.

Every Christian should have at least a basic understanding of these principles. This is true because every believer must have a daily contact with the Word of God. It would be very unwise to hide these skills from church members thinking that they are only for "professional" ministers of the Gospel.

CHAPTER 4

HANDS ON EXEGESIS: THERE AND THEN:

THE HISTORICAL-CULTURAL CONTEXT

One has not completed the task of interpreting a biblical text until he or she has thoroughly addressed the following issues:

- discovering the *historical-cultural context* of the passage,
- understanding the *literary context* of the passage,
- conducting word studies on *key words* in the passage, and
- understanding the *grammatical-structural relationships* within the passage.

It is, therefore, important that we understand each stage of this interpretative process. In this chapter, we will address the first issue, the historical-cultural context. In the next chapter, we will discuss the other three issues.

Investigating the Historical-Cultural Context

The historical-cultural context of a Scripture passage involves all of the human circumstances surrounding the passage, including the cultural context out of which the passage was written. By *cultural context* we mean the ideas, beliefs, and customs that are shared and accepted by people in a society (Summers 2001, 330). This would necessarily include a particular people's way of life, their traditional beliefs, their social forms, their racial traits, and their religious beliefs and practices.

The Bible was written out of the ancient Semitic or Jewish culture of the near East. With few exceptions, this culture is very different from most African cultures. Therefore, most of the cultures found in the Bible are very different from our own culture and way of life. This being true, in order to fully understand a passage of Scripture, the interpreter will be required to dig out the available historical-cultural data. At first, this may seem like hard work, but it will tremendously aid him or her to understand the passage of Scripture. While this historical-cultural information is often hidden beneath the surface, it can be extracted by any serious student of the Bible.

Some have said that, because the Bible is inspired by the Holy Spirit, it is useless to seek to understand the historical-cultural context out of which it was written. In their mind, because the Bible is divinely inspired it transcends all historical and cultural practices and overrides the human limitations of culture. Its interpretation, therefore, cannot be limited by the original author's history and culture.

While this may seem to be true, one should not forget that the Holy Spirit does not manipulate people. Belief in divine inspiration does not excuse us from discovering the cultural, historical, and language differences between the biblical writers and ourselves. The Holy Spirit truly inspired the biblical authors to write God's Word, and today He will illuminate the same Scripture to any Spirit-indwelt interpreter who will earnestly seek the truth. Therefore, with the help of the Holy Spirit the contemporary student of Scripture has the responsibility to "rightly handle the word of truth" (2 Timothy 2:15; compare with 2 Corinthians 4:2).

Knowing the Historical-Cultural Context

Knowing the historical-cultural context out of which a Scripture passage was written helps one to better understand what the biblical author intended to teach. This will in turn help him to more accurately communicate the true meaning of the passage to his or her audience. One great peril of overlooking the historical-cultural context of a passage is the danger of falling into the trap of *eisegesis*, that is, reading into Scripture one's own modern ideas and concepts. As a result, the interpreter—and his audience—miss the true meaning of what was written.

Determining the Historical-Cultural Context

We hear and understand the Bible in much the same way we hear and understand one another in normal conversation. We know the meaning of what is being discussed because we understand the context out of which it is spoken. The same is true in interpreting Scripture. For an interpreter to accurately understand the meaning of a passage, he or she must understand the context out of which the writer is speaking. In other words, one's interpretation must be consistent with the historical-cultural context of the passage. To discover these things, it is essential that the interpreter understand the biblical author, his audience, and the setting out of which he wrote his book. The following three steps will help the interpreter to get started in understanding the historical-cultural context of a biblical passage:

1. Get to Know the Biblical Writer

One must begin by gathering information about the biblical writer himself. Answering the following questions will give the interpreter insight into the author's mission and the circumstances surrounding his work:

- Who was the writer?
- What was his background?
- Where did he come from?
- Where was he when he wrote?
- When did he write?
- What was the nature of his ministry?
- What was his relationship with the people he addressed?
- What prompted him to write?
- What was his purpose in writing?

This knowledge will help the interpreter to better understand the message of the original author.

2. Learn about the Biblical Audience

Knowing the audience to whom a biblical book is written is essential in interpreting Scripture. This includes who the audience is as well as their circumstances at the time of the writing. For example, almost all New Testament epistles are addressed to a particular group of people to address specific issues being faced by the group. The following questions may help the interpreter to arrive at the correct insight about the audience:

- To whom was the book/letter written, that is, who were the original readers?
- What were the circumstances of their lives?
- What was their relationship to God?
- What was their relationship to one another and to the writer of the book?
- What was happening to them at the time of writing?

Knowing these circumstances is an important step in helping one to discover to the right interpretation of the particular text.

3. Understand the General Setting

Finally, the interpreter must have a basic understanding of the setting out of which the biblical author wrote. This would include the local customs, social mores, and religious beliefs of the people. It would also include the political and economic situation surrounding the writing of the book. Further, the meaning of a text may be related to the geographical setting of the passage. It is, therefore, very important that one considers the setting as well.

Bible commentaries and most study Bibles cover much of this background information in the introductory remarks to each book of the Bible. While this is very useful, it is best to research this information from several books before coming to any firm conclusions.

An Example

Let us illustrate what we have just discussed with a quick example from the gospel of John (4:4-38). Understanding of the historical background of the story told in this passage, along with its geographical setting, helps us to better understand and appreciate what it teaches about Jesus and His mission. As the story begins, John states of Jesus, "Now he had to go through Samaria" (v. 4). When one understands the hostility between the Jews and the Samaritans, one will have deeper insights into the significance of Jesus' decision. This inter-tribal hostility between the Jews and Samaritans had to do with how the Samaritans had intermarried with the local pagan people, and how they had set up a rival place of worship to the temple which was in Jerusalem (v. 20). Therefore, Jesus' choosing to go through Samaria took Him through "hostile" territory. He must have had an important reason for going that way instead of taking the normal route along the Jordan River. In this way, understanding the historical, cultural, and geographical background of this passage enhances our understanding of what is actually taking place and what John is trying to teach by telling this story of Jesus. (Additional examples in Appendix A.)

CHAPTER 5

HANDS ON EXEGESIS: THERE AND THEN:

THE LITERARY CONTEXT

In the former chapter, we began our discussion about four important steps in properly interpreting a passage of Scripture. Those four steps are:

- discovering the *historical-cultural context* of the passage,

- understanding the *literary context* of the passage,

- going through word studies on *key words* in the passage and

- understanding the *grammatical-structural* relationships within the passage.

In the previous chapter, we looked at how to discover the historical-cultural context of a passage. In this chapter, we will discuss the remaining three.

The Literary Context

By literary context we mean the words and verses that surround the particular text we are interpreting. Ultimately this context thus includes

- the verses immediately before and after the passage,
- the book in which the passage appears,
- the dispensation in which the passage was written (Old or New Testament), and
- the message of the entire Bible.

The literary context in which a given Scripture passage is contained influences how that passage is to be understood, and thus how it is to be interpreted. Context refers to all that surrounds a given Scripture text. For example, in order to properly interpret Paul's statement in 1 Corinthians 6:12 or 10:23, "Everything is permissible for me—but not everything is beneficial," one must consider its context. If one fails to do this, the passage can be grossly misinterpreted. Does it really mean *everything* is permissible? Is murder, adultery, polygamy and other gross sins permissible to the Christian? These questions are answered when we interpret Paul's statement in its context.

In the case of these two passages quoted, Paul is undoubtedly quoting the theological position of some in the Corinthian congregation who boasted that they had a right to do anything they wished. He confronts the notion by observing that such "freedom" of action may not benefit the Christian in any way. In actual fact, one may just become enslaved by those actions he or she indulges in "at will."

Since God is the Author of Scripture, and since He cannot contradict Himself, no verse of Scripture can mean something contradictory to what is taught in its wider context (Gibbs 2004, 90).

The meaning of the Scripture passage one is reading is determined by the information surrounding the story or text. In order to prove a particular doctrinal point, some have ignored the literary context of a particular passage. As a result, they have drawn meanings out of the text that do not exist. For example, Paul said, "I want to know Christ and the power of his resurrection... becoming like him in his death" (Phil. 3:10, NIV). If one ignores the context of this passage, he or she may erroneously conclude that Paul was still unconverted when he wrote it and that he was seeking to be saved in order that he might know Christ and become like Him. This, of course, is not the case, as the immediate context of this passage, the entire epistle to the Philippians, and the rest of the New Testament reveal. Paul was obviously converted at the time he wrote Philippians 3:10 (Acts 9:1-19; 22:3-16; 26:9-18; Phil. 1:1).

Guidelines for Understanding the Literary Context

Observing a number of guidelines will help us to better understand the literary context of the biblical passage we are seeking to interpret:

1. Consider the main emphasis of the book, chapter and paragraph you are seeking to understand.

2. Answer the following questions about the passage:

    a. What is the thought connection between the given text and the context?

    b. Is the author using any figure of speech that needs to be considered?

    c. Is the text written a response to a particular problem or question?

3. Summarize into one or two sentences all the paragraphs surrounding the text.

4. Identify the complete thought of the larger passage in which the text is found.

5. Look at how thoughts are linked together.

6. Unless you have good reasons to do otherwise, accept the usual and literal sense of the words.

7. Understand that the interpretation of an individual passage must be consistent with the flow of thought of the book in which it is found (Gibbs 2004, 96).

8. Allow Scripture to interpret Scripture and interpret obscure passages in light of clear passages.

Word Studies

According to Scott Duvall and J. Daniel, "Words are like pieces of a puzzle. They fit together to form a story or a paragraph in a letter (i.e., the big picture). Until you know the meaning of certain words, you will not be able to grasp the meaning of the whole passage" (Gibbs 2004, 132). Using another analogy, words are like bricks in a wall. When properly placed together, they bring out the intended meaning of the passage. Once you grasp the meanings of individual words, you are able to put together the meaning of an entire sentence and then of the passage itself. Thus, context helps to determine word meaning just as word meaning helps to form the context.

To properly perform a word study, you must do three things. First, avoid misconceptions about words. Some words are very significant, while others are less so. You must also understand that the Bible versions we use today have all been translated from their original Hebrew, Aramaic or Greek languages. Further, over time some words change their meaning.

Second, to do a proper word study one must focus his or her attention on the key words of the passage being studied. It is not essential to focus on every word in the passage. Word selection is therefore very important. Pay particular attention to those words that are repeated, words that seem to be confusing or ambiguous, and to figures of speech.

Finally, in doing a proper word study, one must seek to understand what the word might most likely mean in the context of the sentence and paragraph in which it is found. It sometimes helps to determine what the word may not mean in the given context. That is to say, context is a decisive factor in determining the meaning of a word.

An Example

The italicized words in the passage below, taken from Paul's letter to the Romans, can serve as a good example of how a word study can help one to discover the author's intended meaning when he first wrote the passage:

> "Therefore, I *urge* you, brothers, in view of God's *mercy*, to *offer* your bodies as *living sacrifices*, holy and pleasing to God—this is your *spiritual act of worship*. Do not *conform* any longer to the *pattern* of this world, but be transformed by the *renewing* of your mind. Then you will be able to *test and approve* what God's will is—His good, pleasing and perfect will" (12:1-2).

Note how this passage contains certain key verbs, nouns, and figures of speech. It also contains some possibly confusing words:

1. Key verbs: urge, offer, conform,
                   transform, renew
2. Key nouns: mercy, pattern

36

3. Figure of speech: living sacrifice
4. Confusing words: spiritual act of worship, test,
                         approve.

In order to properly interpret this passage, the interpreter will need to take time to analyze each of these key words to determine their meaning in the context in which they appear. (Note: For a more comprehensive example, see Appendix E)

Grammatical-Structural Relationships

Further, in interpreting a Scripture passage, one must consider the grammatical and structural relationships within the passage. Grammar is the rules that structure language and give it meaning. It consists of the word forms of a language and their relationships to one another. Without grammar, there can be no language. Hence, understanding the grammatical-structural relationships between words in a passage helps one to better determine its meaning. This is done in four ways:

- by ascertaining the meaning of words (lexicology),

- by understanding the structure of words (morphology),

- by determining the function of words (parts of speech),

- by comparing the relationships of words to one another (syntax).

The grammatical-structural relationships in a passage also help one to understand how the context or setting influences his interpretation of the passage. Therefore, when seeking to determine the grammatical and structural relationships in a passage, one should look for the following:

- repeated words and thoughts,

- contrasting words and thoughts,

- comparisons,

- cause and effect relationships,

- figures of speech (Appendix E),

- parts of speech (such as verbs, nouns, conjunctions, pronouns, etc).

While this process may be similar to doing a word study, as discussed earlier, the actual procedure is different. In analyzing grammar, one must look beyond the individual words and examine the structural relationships between the words, or, how do the words in a passage relate to one another? (Note: An example of how to handle the grammatical-structural relationships within a text is found in Appendix E.).

Bible Versions

When interpreting a passage of Scripture, it is useful to examine it in multiple versions. Each version has its own approach to translation and choice of words translated. A particular version's theory of translation is explained in its introduction at the beginning of the Bible. The serious Bible student will take time to read the introduction of any version of the Bible he or she is using. Further, it is important to understand that earlier translations, like the King James Version, sometimes use dated language. Not understanding this can possibly lead to misunderstandings. Also, take note of any differences in the more literal translations such as the King James Version (KJV), the New King James Version (NKJV), the Revised Standard

Version (RSV), the New American Standard Bible (NASB), and the English Standard Version (ESV). (See Appendix C and D.)

CHAPTER 6

HANDS ON MEANING AND APPLICATION:
HERE AND NOW

The next step in our exegetical processes is to determine the meaning of the passage. Then, and only then, can we apply what we have learned to our own particular context. As we have discussed in previous chapters, this process begins by carefully reading the passage. We then apply the rules of interpretation that will lead us to the correct meaning of the passage (see Appendix E).

Our first interpretative task, then, is to decide what the text meant "there and then." In other words, what meaning did the original author intend to convey to his original readers? Only after doing this can we determine what it means to us "here and now." "There and then" speaks of exegesis; "here and now" speaks of application. Later in this chapter we will discuss the process of application, but first it is necessary that we look a bit more into the issue of *meaning*.

Determining meaning is crucial in the task of biblical interpretation. First and foremost, meaning is determined by what message the original biblical author intended to convey when he first wrote the passage. We call this "authorial intent." Second, and less so, meaning is determined by the response of the original reader(s) of the passage. We are thus saying that meaning is found in the text itself. This being the case, we must guard against speculating about the meaning of the text. We should further avoid allegorizing the text, thus making it say something completely different from what the author intended it to say. Douglas P. Lowenberg asserts, "The original author's intended meaning is the inspired, God-given meaning. This meaning is fixed and cannot be changed. From this meaning found in the words of Scripture, which was given in a specific cultural and historical context, the interpreter establishes principles based on the author's intention" (Lowenberg 2006, 6).

Answering the following questions will help one to determine authorial intent:

- What does this passage mean?
- What was the author's intended meaning?
- What did the text mean to the original audience?
- What are the differences and similarities between the original audience and today's readers?
- What is the theological principle reflected by the text?

Determining the author's intended meaning will, in turn, help the interpreter to find the proper application of the text. Let's now look at how one can best apply the text's theological principles to your own life and to the lives of those you may be ministering to.

The Importance of Application

The task of biblical interpretation is not complete until we apply the meaning of the text to our contemporary context. The laborious task of exegesis is never an end in itself. It is done to find out what God, through His inspired Word, wants to communicate to us today. Lowenberg says, "Biblical studies must move beyond exegesis and hermeneutics to application" (Lowenberg 2006, 18). Elliott E. Johnson adds, "Application is the task of relating what God has said to modern man" (Johnson 1990, 215). The primary reason we study Scripture is so that we might demonstrate loving obedience to our Lord based on the truth revealed in His Word.

Four-Step Method in Application

The following four steps of biblical application will help the interpreter make a proper application of a biblical text to his or her own life and to the lives of their hearers:

1. Determine the original application(s) of the text to the original readers.
2. Evaluate how specifically that application applies to one's present life and audience.
3. Identify any general principles that can apply across time and cultures.
4. Find appropriate applications to the current situation that embody the broader principles taught in the text.

Therefore, when determining application, the interpreter must avoid such follies as neglecting the literary context of the passage and the original intent of the author. He or she must carefully avoid adding their own ideas and ideologies into the mix, or ignoring the text's original intended meaning. They must further avoid making false analogies. Remember, the purpose of the entire exegetical process is to lead the interpreter and his audience to the place of practical application. Application is not the means of the interpretative process but the end. This understanding is most important.

Ultimately, however, the interpreter must always seek to make legitimate application of the true meaning of text.

The Role of the Holy Spirit

The illumination of the Holy Spirit is crucial in biblical interpretation. The Bible tells us that "all Scripture is inspired by God" (2 Tim. 3:16). This inspiration came through the agency of Holy Spirit, for the writers of Scripture "spoke from God as they were carried along by the Holy Spirit" (2 Pet. 1:21). Inspiration was thus the work of Holy Spirit in and through the lives of the prophets and apostles producing the very "word of God" (1 Thess. 2:13). God Himself was communicating through them to mankind (Heb. 1:1).

The same Holy Spirit who inspired Scripture is still at work in the lives of Spirit-indwelt believers illuminating the text to them. He is available to help interpreters discern the truth of Scripture as well as apply to its truths to their own lives and the lives of those to whom they are ministering. The theological term for this work of the Spirit is *illumination*. Since the Holy Spirit is the one who inspired Scripture, it is logical to assume that He is its best interpreter. We must therefore seek His presence and trust Him to guide us as we interpret Scripture today.

This is not to say that the interpreter has no personal responsibility in the process. As we have contended throughout this work, he or she must employ the correct hermeneutical tools. The Holy Spirit does not illuminate outside of the interpreter's own efforts in understanding the text. The Spirit works with the interpreter as he or she follows the correct

43

principles of interpretation. He then helps to guide them into the right conclusions and applications.

There is no such a thing as "new revelation." That is, there are no new interpretations or meanings that have never before existed and are now unveiled to us by the Holy Spirit. The Spirit does not create new meanings that were never intended by the original authors of Scripture. He, rather, helps us to understand and apply what was originally revealed to the biblical authors.

CHAPTER 7

AN EXAMPLE OF BIBLICAL INTERPRETATION

Interpreting 1 Timothy 5:17-20

The elders who direct the affairs of the church well are worthy of double honour, especially those whose work is preaching and teaching. ¹⁸For the Scripture says, "Do not muzzle the ox while it is treading out the grain," and "The worker deserves his wages." ¹⁹Do not entertain an accusation against an elder unless it is brought by two or three witnesses. ²⁰Those who sin are to be rebuked publicly, so that the others may take warning. (NIV)

In this appendix, I will seek to provide an example of how one may go about interpreting a passage of Scripture. By observing this procedure, the reader will gain insight on how this may be done on other passages as well. It follows six steps:

1. Surveying the general historical context
2. Creating an annotated outline
3. Determining the limits of the passage
4. Examining the sentence structure
5. Reviewing the broader biblical and theological contexts
6. Making the final presentation

Surveying the General Historical Context

Author and Recipients

The writer of the paragraph is Paul, the apostle of Jesus Christ, set apart by the will of God and the Lord Jesus Christ. He was writing to Timothy, whom he calls his own son (1:2). Timothy had found Christ as a result of Paul's missionary ministry in Galatia and had served with him in the gospel (Phil. 2:22). Timothy was a native of Lystra (modern Turkey). His father was a Greek and his mother was a Jewish Christian named Eunice. He joined Paul's missionary team during Paul's second missionary journey (Acts 16:1-4). He had been delegated by Paul as his representative to carry out special apostolic tasks. Timothy is presented as a dear friend of Paul and a faithful, diligent worker (Phil. 2:19-20).

Purpose

On his way to Macedonia, Paul had left Timothy in Ephesus to take care of the church there (1 Timothy 1:3). He wanted Timothy to deal with the false teachings beginning to proliferate there (1:3). After he had arrived in Macedonia, Paul realized that it would to be difficult for him return to Ephesus any time soon (3:14-15). He, therefore, wrote this 1 Timothy to give guidance to the young minister. On one hand, Paul charged Timothy to be an exemplary individual (1:3-7, 18-20; 4:6-16; 6:11-21). On the other hand, he advised him in matters concerning the leadership of the church and how deal with false teachings (1:3; 3:1-14; 4:6-16). In the midst of addressing these issues he also explains how faithful leaders ought to be treated by their members.

Repeated Words

Our chosen passage is found in the context of repeated instructions concerning the qualifications and exercise of church leadership. These words "elders," "work" and "honour" are mentioned regularly. These three words, therefore, deserve special attention.

1. Elder. The Greek word translated "elder" in this passage is *presbuteros*. It carries the connotation (or comparative) of *presbus*, meaning an elderly or older person. Figuratively, it could mean a member of the celestial council or a Christian "presbyter."

2. Honour. The Greek word translated "honour" here means a precious price. It speaks of value placed upon, or the money paid for, something valuable. By analogy it means the high esteem given to a person, or the dignity that person possesses.

3. Work. The Greek word translated "toil" in this passage is *kopiao*. It means to feel fatigue, and by implication, to work hard (Biblesoft's 1994).

Creating an Annotated Outline (5:17-20)

At this point it is useful to construct an annotated outline of the passage we are interpreting. This will enable us to look more closely into the texts.

5:17. Here Paul identifies elders as spiritual leaders called to direct church affairs. They fulfill their ministry through preaching and teaching. Those elders who perform these noble tasks in a godly and fruitful manner are to be given "double honour." This double honour includes regular honoraria (money), material blessings, and personal and family care by members.

5:18. Paul uses the analogy of oxen employed to tread out grain

47

to illustrate this care. He notes how even dumb oxen are allowed to freely feed on the grain while they work. The more they work, the more they eat. In like manner, elders who faithfully perform their work are worthy of their wages and should be generously rewarded for their labor.

5:19. Another way that members should give double honour to faithful elders is to refuse to receive unsubstantiated accusations against them. Any accusation against an elder must be attested to by two or more witnesses (v. 17). Elders are thus protected from disciplinary investigations arising from mere gossip.

5:20. In cases where church leaders are truly guilty of serious sin, and they persist in that sin, they should be publically rebuked. This should be done "so that the others may take warning." Such a warning would help others to avoid similar sin and to live lives of holiness. It is possible that Paul gleaned this principle from his study of the Law of Moses (Deut. 19:15).

It is important to understand that our chosen passage—along with any other passage being interpreted—does not stand alone. It must be interpreted in light of what has been discussed in other passages concerning the church leaders and the way they discharge their ministry. In summary, while church leaders who faithfully fulfill their calling should be honoured, false teachers who travel from church to church spreading falsity should be dealt with harshly (Biblesoft's 1994).

Examining the Sentence Structure

Below is an example taken 1 Timothy 5:17 and 20, showing how this passage of Paul may be structured. Such structuring helps the interpreter to see the relationships of the words and thoughts in the passage.

> 17 well direct the affairs elders
>
> of double honour
>
> especially those whose work
>
> is preaching and teaching
>
> 20 Do not accuse
>
> Those (elders) who sin
>
> be rebuked
>
> others may take warning

Reviewing the Broader Biblical and Theological Contexts

One can broaden his or her biblical and theological insight into a passage by examining what commentaries have to say. Below are two quotations from the PC Study Bible, version 3.0, that give insight into passage.

Quotation 1: "Of double honour. An old and common contract adjective *diploos*, two-fold, in opposition to *haploos*, single fold. But why 'of double honour'? See 1 Tim. 6:1 for 'of all honour.' White suggests 'remuneration' rather than 'honour' for *timees* (a common use for price or pay). Liddon proposes 'honorarium' (both honour and pay and so 'double'). Wetstein gives numerous examples of soldiers receiving double pay for unusual services. Some suggest twice the pay given the enrolled widows" (Robertson's 1997).

Quotation 2: "Double honour *diplees timees*. This at least includes pecuniary remuneration for services, if it is not limited to that. The use of *timee* as 'pay or price' appears Matt. 27:6, 9; Acts 4:34; 7:16; 1 Cor. 6:20. 'Double,' not in a strictly literal sense, but as *pleiona timeen* 'more honour,' Heb 3:3. The comparison is with those elders who do not exhibit equal capacity or efficiency in ruling. This is a principle of respecting leaders in the church.

Making the Final Presentation

In summary, Paul taught three things regarding church leaders in our passage.[1] They are to be materially supported; they are to be protected from unsubstantiated accusations; and those who persist in sin are to be disciplined accordingly. These three practices are to be performed out of an attitude of genuine concern for church leaders (vv. 17-19). They deserve "double honour," which includes both material support and appropriate vocal approbation.

A congregation should consider it an honour to have a pastor who works hard in preaching and teaching the Word of God, leading the church in prayer, and ensuring proper pastoral care.

---

[1] I am using the word "church leaders" in place of "elders" because of the limitations and implications it has in our days. In many contexts, the word is limited to deacons only. Rarely this is used for pastors.

The pastor should also consider it a privilege to lead a local church in these areas. Since leading a congregation is already an honoured role, it becomes a double honour when he or she is adequately remunerated for the privilege. Double honour does not mean double pay, meaning the "teaching pastor" gets twice as much salary as those who serve in other capacities. Rather, it means "twofold honour," the honour due those in such positions as well as their normal financial remunerations.

Not only should those who serve well be adequately remunerated, those pastors who are accused of wrongdoing should be honoured by being given the benefit of the doubt until adequate evidence of their sin is produced. When one does sin, and refuses to acknowledge his sin and repent, and when one is found guilty of wrongdoing, he or she should be rebuked publicly.

CHAPTER 8

GENERAL HERMENEUTICAL PRINCIPLES

Sometimes, in order to grasp a concept, it is essential that we see all of its constituent parts together at one time. This chapter will therefore present a broad overview of the hermeneutical principles needed for one to "correctly handle the word of truth" (2 Tim. 2:15). Those ten principles are as follows:

1. The literal interpretation principle
2. The contextual principle
3. The Scripture interprets Scripture principle
4. The progressive revelation principle
5. The unity in diversity principle
6. The one interpretation principle
7. The harmony of Scripture principle
8. The genre principle
9. The grammatical principle
10. The historical background principle

We will now look at each of these common sense interpretative principles: (See also Appendix B).

The Literal Interpretation Principle

Applying the literal interpretation principle is foundational to a correct understanding of Scripture. This principle says that when the direct sense of the Scripture makes sense, do not seek a different sense. One should, therefore, first seek to know the primary, evident meaning of the text—unless the immediate context, studied in the light of related passages and basic truths, clearly indicates otherwise. Further, one must be aware that figures of speech, such as symbols and allegories, are to be interpreted in light of the more obvious, literal meaning of the text. In other words, figurative language is to be interpreted in the light of explicit language, and not the other way round.

The Contextual Principle

As previously discussed in this book, context refers to all that surrounds a particular passage of Scripture. Ultimately, that context includes all of Scripture. Since the Word of God is inspired by one Divine Author, the Holy Spirit, it is woven together into a single unit. This unity can be traced from beginning to end. More particularly, it is essential that the interpreter considers the verses immediately surrounding the passage being interpreted. If Bible interpreters would consistent apply the contextual principle, this one thing would go a long way in ensuring a correct understanding of Scripture. A text must *always* be understood in the light of its context. Or, as one scholar said, "A text without its context can quickly become a pretext."

The Scripture Interprets Scripture Principle

A related principle to the one above is that Scripture interprets Scripture. It goes without saying that biblical truth can only be found in the Bible itself, and that no biblical truth can be found outside of its pages. Further, since the Bible has been completed, we can expect no new revelation. It is therefore essential that we understand that the Bible is its own inter-preter. As noted earlier, when drawing a meaning from similar

53

passages, study the context of the two passages to see if they are discussing a similar subject, and remember, the clearer passage must be used to guide the interpretation of the more obscure passage.

The Progressive Revelation Principle

Beginning with the story of creation to the end of the Bible, one great theme dominates the Word of God, that is, the redemption of mankind. The Bible's revelation of this theme is progressive. This means that God did not reveal His entire plan all at once. He rather revealed it progressively over a long period of time. This means that we must always interpret any given passage of Scripture in light of the big story of redemption. This can be done best using the biblical theological approach to Scripture rather than the systematic theology approach.

The Unity in Diversity Principle

In interpreting Scripture one must keep in mind the principle of diversity. While the Bible has one dominating theme, that one theme has been revealed in the context of great diversity. The infinite God revealed divine truth to finite man over a period of about 1,500 years. This He did through about forty human authors who wrote out of multiple cultures in three human languages, Hebrew, Aramaic, and Greek. God thus made Himself and His redemptive purposes known to mankind in a diverse yet unified way. Anyone seeking to interpret Scripture would do well to keep this in mind.

The One Interpretation Principle

The one interpretation principle states that every Scripture passage, although it may have multiple applications, has only one true interpretation. It therefore cannot mean on thing to one interpreter and another thing to another interpreter. The one correct interpretation is that which accurately reflects the original intent of the inspired author. The goal of the Bible scholar, then, is to find that "one" interpretation through the illumination of the Holy Spirit and the application of sound hermeneutical methods.

The Harmony of Scripture Principle

The harmony of Scripture principle is based on the fact that all of Scripture has been divinely revealed by the one infallible God. Therefore, the Bible does not—in fact, it cannot—contradict itself. The Almighty God revealed Himself perfectly to mankind, and everything written in the Bible is in complete harmony with everything else. Therefore, any apparent conflict or contradiction can be resolved through a proper application of sound hermeneutical principles.

The Genre Principle

The genre principle recognizes the fact that the Bible was written in several literary *genres*. A genre is a type or category of literature. The wise interpreter of Scripture must therefore be aware of the genre of the specific portion of Scripture he or she is interpreting and must deal with it according to its own rules and norms of interpretation. They must ask such questions as, "Are we dealing with poetry or prose?" and "Are we dealing with history or prophecy?" It is important that, when we are interpreting the Word of God, we understand as much as possible the author's intent and the genre in which he is writing. The Bible contains at least nine literary genres, five in the Old Testament and four in the new as follows:

Old Testament:

1. Historical Narrative: Non-fiction stories of God's dealing with mankind

2. Law: God's commands

3. Poetry: Psalms and songs

4. Wisdom Literature: Wise sayings

5. Prophecy: God speaking to Israel and the nations through His prophets

New Testament:

1. Gospels: Biography and history of Jesus' life and ministry
2. Historical Narratives: The beginning and spread of Jesus' ministry through the apostles and early disciples
3. Epistles: Teaching and doctrine from apostles to the church
4. Apocalyptic Literature (Revelation): Eschatology and Prophecy

The student of Scripture must ever keep in mind that each genre of literature in the Bible requires its own approach to interpretation.

The Grammatical Principle

The grammatical principle of interpretation recognizes that language is governed by certain grammatical rules, and that, when interpreting Scripture, the interpreter must understand and apply these rules. While in the English language we have several highly accurate translations of the Bible, all translations reflect a certain level of interpretation on the part of the translators. Thus, the study of word meanings, grammar, and syntax of the original languages is required for a proper understanding of Scripture. This does not mean that every student of the Bible must learn Hebrew or Greek. Although such understanding of the biblical languages is certainly an added advantage, the English speaker can utilize lexicons, Bible dictionaries, and detailed exegetical commentaries to help them better understand Scripture.

The Historical Background Principle

Every book in the Bible was written from within a specific culture at a particular time in history. While all Scripture is universal in application, its truths can be fully understood and applied only when one takes into account the cultural and historical context out of which it was written. For example, when Paul talks about the meaning and purpose of a woman covering her head in worship (1 Cor. 11:14-15), we can better understand what he was trying to accomplish if we understand the Jewish tradition and religious practice of first-century diaspora Judaism. The same can be said about many other passages of Scripture. It is therefore very important that one understands and applies the historical background principle when he or she is interpreting Scripture.

Imagine what would happen if we would consistently apply these ten key hermeneutical principles when seeking to find the true meaning of Scripture—that is, the author's original intended meaning. It would help to ensure that we are rightfully dividing the word of truth.

Appendix A:
EXAMPLES OF HISTORICAL-CULTURAL CONTEXT

(Taken and adjusted from: http://servantofmessiah.org/wp-content/uploads/downloads/2012/11/Hermeneutics-Course-College-Notes.pdf Accessed on 14th July 2015)

How do various cultural customs affect the interpretation of certain passages?

The four categories of culture include thoughts and beliefs, speech, actions, and artifacts. These four categories may be further divided into fourteen (sometimes overlapping) subcategories. What one thinks influences what he does, and what he does relates back to what he believes, and so it goes.

Following are some examples of Bible passages whose interpretation is affected by the interpreter's knowledge (or lack of knowledge) of aspects of the cultural context out of which they were written.

A. *Political (national, international and civil matters)*

1. Example: Jonah's reluctance to go to Nineveh

   "The Ninevites were atrocious in the way they treated their enemies ... No wonder Jonah did not want to preach a message of repentance to the Ninevites! He felt they deserved judgment for their atrocities" (Zuck 1991, 81).

2. Example: Third position in Babylon (Daniel 5:7, 16)

"Why did King Belshazzar offer Daniel the third position in his kingdom and not the second? The reason is that Belshazzar was only second in command himself. His father, Nabonidus, was actually first in command though he was temporarily out of the country" (Vlach)

3. Example: The Samaritans

"Understanding who the Samaritans were will help one's understanding of the gospels. The Samaritans were descendants of the Jews who remained in Palestine after the Assyrians defeated Israel. They came from mixed marriages between Jews and Assyrian settlers who entered the Promised Land. They also set up their own worship system where they built their own temple and sacrificed animals. Because of their mixed heritage and worship system, they were despised by the Jews. Understanding Jewish hatred for Samaritans helps us understand the significance of Jesus' willingness to speak to a Samaritan woman (John 4), the story of the Good Samaritan (Luke 10:25-37) and the account of the Samaritan leper who returned to give Jesus thanks (Luke 17:11-19) (Packer, Merrill C. Tenney and William White 1980).

B. *Religious*

1. Example: Corban in Mark 7

"In Mark 7 ... Jesus upbraids the Pharisees soundly for their concept of corban. In the practice of corban, a man could declare that all his money would go to the temple treasury when he died, and that, since his money belonged to God, he was therefore no longer responsible for maintaining his aging parents. Jesus argues that men were using the Pharisaic tradition to render God's command (the fifth commandment) of no account. Without a knowledge of the cultural practice of corban, we would be unable to understand this passage" (Virkler 1981, 79).

2. Example: Meat sacrificed to idols in 1 Corinthians 8

"What was the point of meat being sacrificed to idols which Paul discussed in 1 Corinthians 8? No one today sits down to a meal in the home of a guest and asks if the meat had been sacrificed to idols. Obviously this custom pertained to a cultural setting different from today. The point is that people in Corinth would buy meat in the marketplace, offer some of it to pagan idols in one of several temples, and then take the rest of it home for dinner. Therefore, some Christians felt that eating such meat involved them in idol worship" (Zuck 1991, 94).

3. Example: Elijah, Baal and Mount Carmel (1 Kings 18)

"Why did Elijah choose Mount Carmel as the place for his showdown with the 450 prophets of Baal? The followers of Baal believed that Mount Carmel was the home of Baal. Showing the supremacy of Yahweh on Baal's home turf would be devastating to the followers of Baal" (Vlach) Baal was the fire and lightening god.

C. *Economic*

1. Example: Giving of a sandal

"Why did Elimelech's closest relative give his sandal to Boaz? (Ruth 4:8, 17). According to the Nuzi tablets, (Nuzi 1937, 53-56). discovered in present-day Iraq, in excavations from 1925-1931, such an action symbolized releasing one's right to land he walked on. This was done when a sale of land was completed" (Zuck 1991, 84).

2. Example: How much is a "denarius"? (Rev. 6:6)

"A denarius is one day's wage. In Revelation 6:6 famine conditions will be so bad that a full day of work will barely be enough for a man to feed his family" (Vlach).

D. *Legal*

1. Example: The Stolen Blessing

"In Genesis 27, Jacob deceives his father, Isaac, and receives the blessing that was supposed to be for Esau. When the plot was discovered, Isaac could not change the result. Why? It might seem strange to members of Western society that such importance was placed on an oral blessing or testament. However, recent discoveries have verified that an oral benediction (in those days) was legally as valid as a written last will and testament" (Vlach).

2. Example: Daniel, Darius and the lion's den (Daniel 6)

"When King Darius of Medo-Persia was tricked into making a decree that would send Daniel to the lion's den, why didn't he simply revoke his former decree since he wanted Daniel to live (Dan. 6:14)? Once a decree was made in this empire, no one, not even the king, could revoke it (see Esther 8:8)" (Vlach).

3. Example: Elisha's Request for a Double Blessing

    In 2 Kings 2:9 did Elisha want twice as much spiritual power as Elijah had? This question can be solved by Deuteronomy 21:17 and the double portion of the inheritance that the firstborn received.

E. *Agricultural*

    "The Jewish involvement with the land was reflected in the teachings of Jesus Christ. His imagery and illustrations gave His listeners vivid pictures, such as a sower, pouch at his side, flinging seed across a newly plowed field. He frequently used metaphors about rich ripe grapes and fruitful vines" (Coleman 1987).

1. Example: The Fig tree (Mark 11:12-14)

    "Why did Jesus denounce a fig tree for having no fruit when it was not even the season for figs? In March fig trees in Israel normally produce small buds followed by large green leaves in April. The small buds were edible 'fruit.' The time when Jesus 'cursed' the fig tree was the Passover, that is, April. Since the tree had no buds it would bear no fruit that year. But 'the season for figs' was late May and June, when the normal crops of figs ripened. Jesus' denouncing of the tree symbolized Israel's absence of spiritual vitality (like the absence of the buds) in spite of her outward religiosity (like green leaves)" (Zuck 1991, 86).

2. Example: Vines and the Vineyard

"The vine was of great importance in the religion of Israel. It was used as a symbol of the religious life of Israel itself, and a carving of a bunch of grapes often adorned the front exterior of a synagogue. The symbolism was based upon passages such as Psalm 80 and Isaiah 5:1-5 where Israel is God's vine. The importance of the vine is why the Pharisees took the point so angrily when Jesus told the story of the wicked tenants in the vineyard (Matthew 21:33-41, 45-46)" (Gower, 111).

3. Example: Samuel's Request for Rain

"What is so unusual about Samuel calling on the Lord for rain at the time of the wheat harvest in I Samuel 12:17? Because from April to October there was no rain. It would be like calling for snow in July and August in South California" (Lewis, 12/2006).

4. Example: Why did Amos call the women of Bethel "cows of Bashan" in Amos 4:1?

"Bashan area in NE Israel was very fertile and the cows do not have to struggle to eat but instead become fat and lazy" (Vlach).

5. Example: Mustard Seed

"Why did Jesus call the mustard seed the smallest seed in Matthew 13:31-32? Was this a botanical error? In one year, it could grow 15-30 feet. Of those that were planted in that area it was the smallest known of that day (the orchid seed is smaller)" (Lewis, 12/2006).

F. *Architectural*

"How could four men let a paralytic man down through a roof? (Mark 2:1-12) Most houses in the Western world are built with slanted roofs, but in Bible times roofs were flat and often were made of tiles. Therefore, it would be no problem for these men to stand on the roof, remove some of the tiles, and let the man down" (Zuck 1991, 86).

G. *Clothing*

"What is meant by the command 'Gird up your loins' in Job 38:3; 40:7; and 1 Peter 1:13? When a man ran, worked, or was in battle, he would tuck his robe under a wide sash at his waist so that he could move about more easily. The command thus means to be alert and capable of responding quickly" (Zuck 1991, 86).

H. *Domestic*

1. "Burying the Father – In Luke 9:59 a man who wanted to be Jesus' disciple wanted to first bury his father. Was Jesus' denial of this request insensitive? Actually, to bury one's father meant to wait until one's father died (which could take years) so one could receive his inheritance. Thus, Jesus' denial stressed the urgency of following Him immediately" (Vlach)

2. "John's leaning on Jesus at the Last Supper (John 13:23). Back then people did not sit in chairs at meals as we do

today. They were either on the floor or on couches. To lean on someone, then, was not considered rude" (Vlach)

I. *Geographical*

1. Example: Passing through Samaria

"What was significant about Jesus passing through Samaria (John 4)? The Jews would not defile themselves by walking through the land of the Samaritans, who the Jews considered half-breeds. Jesus would not partake in this prejudice" (Vlach).

2. Example: Lukewarm water

"In Revelation 3:16 the church at Laodicea was referred to as 'lukewarm.' This undoubtedly is a play on the lukewarm water the people had in that city. The water in Laodicea was channeled six miles from Hieropolis. When the water left Hieropolis, it was hot, but by the time it reached Laodicea, it was lukewarm" (Vlach).

3. Example: Going down from Jerusalem

"Why did Jesus speak of a man going 'down' from Jerusalem to Jericho when Jericho is located northeast of Jerusalem? (Luke 10:30) The elevation drop in the 14 miles from Jerusalem to Jericho is more than 2,000 feet. Obviously going from Jerusalem to Jericho then was to go down in elevation" (Zuck 1991, 86).

J. *Social*

1. Example: Mourners

"Why when Jesus went to the house where a little girl had died, were there flute-players and a noisy crowd (Matt. 9:23)? It was the custom then that when a person died, the family would hire professional mourners to show how much they cared for their lost loved one" (Vlach)

2. Example: Sackcloth and ashes

"The Israelites used sackcloth as a ritual sign of repentance or a token of mourning ... The New Testament also associates sackcloth with repentance (see Matt. 11:21). The sorrowful Israelite would clothe himself in sackcloth, place ashes upon his head, and then sit in the ashes. Our modern Western custom of wearing dark colors to funerals corresponds to the Israelites' gesture of wearing sackcloth" (Parker 1971).

3. Example: Why did Paul say in II Corinthians 2:14 that Christ "leads us in His triumph in Christ"?

"TRIUMPHUS, a solemn procession in which a victorious general entered the city in a chariot drawn by four horses. He was preceded by the captives and spoils taken in war, was followed by his troops, and after passing in state along the Via Sacra, ascended the Capitol to offer sacrifice in the temple of Jupiter" (Ramsay 1875, 1163-1167).

A SUMMARY OF GENERAL HERMENEUTICAL PRINCIPLES
(Douglas P. Lowenberg, 2006)

1. The biblical author determined the meaning of the text. The idea or instruction he intended to communicate by his selection of words and genre is the inspired meaning of the text.

2. The Holy Spirit inspired the message and enabled the author to communicate God's message accurately without diluting or neglecting any essential components of the content.

3. The author consciously willed to communicate his God-inspired message to his audience, choosing words that had a common meaning to him and the reader, so that the recipients could understand it and respond appropriately.

4. The meaning of the text does not change. What it meant it still means. A text cannot mean what it never meant.

5. The meaning is found in the words that were written. The message is encoded in the words selected by the author. Words have a range of meanings which is called the "norms of language." However, when an author employs the words in the construction of a sentence and thought, he designates a specific meaning to the word. The meaning is called the "norms of utterance." The hermeneutist must prioritize the words of the text within their literary context as he seeks to discover the author's meaning rather than allowing what is learned from the historical, cultural and spiritual context to

overshadow the common sense meaning of the written text. He cannot allow the historical context to create an unnatural or inconsistent meaning for the words.

6. The meaning of a text may have implications, a pattern of meaning established by the words of the author which goes beyond the specifics of what he consciously willed. Some refer to an implication as the author's unconscious meaning. It legitimately falls within the pattern of meaning willed by the author but addressed a wider situation than he specifically addressed. Implications are controlled and limited by the writer's meaning. Extended implications that exceed the author's intent must be avoided.

7. Mental acts are what the author may have thought and experienced during the time that he wrote the inspired text but were not conveyed in the words of the text. Mental acts fall within the category of the private domain of the author and are not accessible to the reader. Delving into this realm is purely speculative. The written message is in the public domain, available to the reader, and is the inspired data that one should analyze in order to find the author's meaning and the God-breathed message.

8. Subject matter is the wide variety of issues to which the author referred as he wrote but is not the purpose for writing the text.

   • For example, he may have referred to a city wall but his willed meaning was not to address ancient wall construction. A reference to the Jordan River was not intended to provide an analysis on the length, depth or animal life associated with the river. The record of the appearance of an angel was not intended to teach on the nature, height or physical features of a heavenly being.

9. Everyone approaches the Word of God with a mind and understanding that has been influenced by his/her worldview, culture, experience, religious tradition and sin. He must recognize the biases and presuppositions he brings to the text and attempt to neutralize their influences. He must allow the biblical author to speak supremely and judge his/her worldview, culture and agenda.

   • For example, one person stated that the Bible is written by leaders to leaders about leadership. He said that one does injustice to the text if he does not recognize this leadership perspective. Are these assumptions valid?

10. There is a two-step process to exposing the meaning of the text to one's audience: the first step is called exegesis, while the second is called hermeneutics. Exegesis finds what the text meant to the original author in his historical context. Hermeneutics states that same meaning in the form of a universal, timeless principle or pattern of meaning that is relevant to one's contemporary audience.

11. Exegesis must precede hermeneutics. One must remember that the text was theirs (the original author's and his audience) before it was ours.

12. When doing exegesis, one must consider five contexts simultaneously in order to uncover the author's meaning.

The first three are aspects of the literary context; the other two are dimensions of the historical context.

a. The "immediate literary context" refers to the words, phrases, sentences and paragraphs that make up the text. One cannot separate a word or phrase from its immediate context without doing damage to the author's meaning.

b. The second aspect of literary context is the "genre," the type or style or writing used by the author to convey his message. Genre consists of form, content and the intended impact of the message on the readers.

c. The third aspect of literary context is the "distant literary context" which can also be called the "hermeneutical circle." It refers to the message of one text as compared to other things said about that subject written by the same author or else in Scripture. It assumes that the entire Bible was inspired by God and that the Bible does not contradict itself. It encourages the exegete to allow Scripture to interpret Scripture, and the more obscure passage to be explained by the text that is more explicit and clear.

d. The first aspect of historical context is the "general historical context" which considers the author, setting, date of writing, audience, relationship between author and audience, purpose for writing, and the cultural, social and spiritual dynamics of the recipients.

e. The second aspect of the historical context is the "immediate historical context." One must seek to understand what specific issue is being addressed by the passage that is under consideration.

13. The second step of interpretation, hermeneutics, requires that each one examines the text within its five contexts to establish the author's intended meaning. From that meaning the exegete can determine principles that maintain the author's meaning while stating it in a relevant manner for his/her contemporary audience. One must be careful to consider the role of cultural relativity. He must look for the meaning that is clearly supra-cultural and transcends cultural particulars.

14. One must be aware of "similar particulars" when comparing the context of the passage with one's contemporary setting. When the exegete's life setting is genuinely similar to the life setting of the biblical author and his audience, God's Word is easily understood and directly applicable. However, when the contemporary situation is different, one must be careful about establishing principles and making application. This is true both when one's situation is clearly and radically different, and when one's situation looks similar but the meaning of cultural and spiritual forms has meanings that differ from the biblical setting.

- For example, how does the circumcision issue in Africa today, for men or for women, compare with the required circumcision for those entering the Abrahamic covenant or with the problem discussed in Galatians 5:2-12?

- How does God view polygamy according to the OT?

- Should a Christian believer deal with a sorcerer or medium in the same way that God instructed in the OT law?

- Are there contemporary situations where Christians have to guard against eating food that has been devoted to idolatrous or ancestral spirits (1 Cor. 8-10)?

- Is the meaning and purpose of head coverings in contemporary Africa the same as Paul discussed in 1 Corinthians 11:14, 15?

- Are the ethical standards of the Old and New Testaments anachronistic for Christians in Africa?

- Are local believers getting drunk at the Lord's Table (1 Cor. 11:17-22)? Is there a contemporary counterpart to this issue?

- When a "man of God" imparts his anointing upon his followers, is he doing the same thing as Moses did (Num. 11:16-17)?

15. The goal of interpretation is to find the plain, common sense meaning of the text that the author intended and consciously communicated rather than pursuing a unique, creative (allegorical) meaning.

16. Each text has only one meaning, the meaning the author intended to be understood by his readership. Normally the author communicated in a clear, unambiguous manner. If he

intended to be ambiguous, his intended (ambiguous) meaning is still the one meaning of the text.

17. The hermeneutist must decide if the author intended his message to be read literally or figuratively. His meaning is expressed through his intended message. To ignore the nature of the message, whether literal or figurative, is to misinterpret the author's meaning.

18. The authors used commissive and referential language. Commissive means that the message includes expressions of emotions and seeks to elicit a response from the reader. The language contains figurative, metaphorical references. It is not to be interpreted literally as though it communicated with scientific accuracy. Referential language is precise and descriptive, aimed at one's cognition. It is intended to inform. While these two are not mutually exclusive, one must be aware of the author's intentions for using a certain type of language.

19. At times an author used idioms. Idioms had a clear intent, a specific meaning, but the author used words in a way which varied from their normal sense. He assumed the reader would understand. One example has to do with "love-hate" terminology. See

• Mal 1:2-3; Gen. 29:30-31; Prov. 13:24

• In each of these cases, love and hate should not be taken literally but the words are intended to show a contrast: one object is loved much more than another; the one "hated" is loved less rather than loathed. Both can still be loved.

20. Some authors used hyperbole, intentional and purposeful exaggeration. The purpose was to emphasize something by overstatement. For example, see

- 2 Sam. 1:23 and Jer. 6:13.

21. "Understanding" occurs for the reader when he mentally grasps what the author intended to communicate.

22. After the meaning is ascertained, the reader personally assigns value to the author's intentions. The value he gives the text and the attitude with which he reverses the meaning is called "significance." One may understand the meaning correctly but determine that its message is irrelevant to himself and disregard its implications.

23. The reader becomes the "interpreter" of the text when, after grasping the meaning, he expresses what he understands as the author's meaning to someone else.

24. While each text has one fixed meaning, there are many applications (with a limited range [*my addition*]).

25. Three good questions to ask of every text:

- What does the text mean (content)?

- Why was the text written (purpose)?

- Why is this text is placed here (literary context)?

26. The more obscure a text is (a text which has an unclear meaning for the contemporary exegete and an unclear historical, cultural and spiritual context), the less dogmatically one should hold his/her interpretation.

Appendix C: Translation Theory
(T. David Gordon, 1985)

While not everyone who drives an automobile needs to understand the theory behind the internal combustion engine, *someone* does need to know this theory. I may be able to drive my Pontiac without any knowledge of internal combustion engines, until the Pontiac breaks down. Then, I must find someone (presumably a mechanic) who does in fact know enough theory to get the Pontiac running again.

The same is true of translation theory. It is not necessary for everyone to know translation theory, nor is it even necessary for pastors and teachers to know *everything* about translation theory. It is necessary for pastors and teachers in the American church at the end of the twentieth century to know *something* about translation theory, for two reasons. First, it will affect the way we interpret the Bible for our people. If we are completely unaware of translation theory, we may unwittingly mislead our brothers and sisters in our interpretation. Second, there are so many English translations available, that no contemporary pastor will be able to escape the inevitable questions about which translations are superior.

It is not my intention to provide anything like an exhaustive approach to either translation theory or semantic theory (relax, I'll define this word later). Rather, I intend to discuss briefly the more important observations, which may be useful to the pastoral ministry.

1. Communication has three parties.

Translation theory shares a number of concerns with what is commonly called *communication theory*. Perhaps the most important observation which the communication theorists have produced for translators is the recognition that *every act of communication has three dimensions*: Speaker (or author), Message, and Audience. The more we can know about the original author, the actual message produced by that author, and the original audience, the better acquainted we will be with that particular act of communication. An awareness of this tri-partite character of communication can be very useful for interpreters. Assuming that an act of communication is right now taking place, as you read what I wrote, there are three dimensions to this particular act of communication: myself, and what I am intending to communicate; the actual words which are on this page; and what you understand me to be saying. When the three dimensions converge, the communication has been efficient.

If we know, perhaps from another source, what an individual author's circumstances are, this may help us understand the actual message produced. Martin Luther King, Jr.'s "Letters from Prison" are better understood by someone who knows the circumstances under which they were written rather than by someone who is oblivious to mid-20th century American history. If we know information about the author's audience, this may also help us to understand the message itself. John Kennedy's famous, "Ich bin ein Berliner" speech is better understood if one understands the apprehensions which many West German citizens had about American foreign policy during the early

1960s (and, knowing the audience was German may help explain why he did not speak this sentence in English!).

Recognizing that in addition to the message itself, there are the two other components of author and audience, the interpreter attempts to uncover as much information as possible about the author and audience. This is why biblical scholars spend so much time attempting to locate the circumstances of a given epistle; they are trying to discover information about author and audience, which will help complete the understanding of the particular act of communication represented by the message.

At this point, an important warning needs to be expressed. For students of literature whose original audience and author are not present (i.e., dead), we only have direct access to one of the three parties in the communicative process: the message itself. Whereas we would be profited by having direct access to author and audience ("Paul, what in the world did you mean about baptizing for the dead?"; or, "How did it hit you Galatians when Paul said he wished his troublers would castrate themselves?"), it would be incorrect to suggest that we must have such access for any understanding to take place. Frequently one encounters the extravagant statement to the effect that "one cannot understand a biblical book unless one understands the author's (or audience's) circumstances." The problem with such statements is that they imply that we can have no understanding without access to information which simply does not always exist. We haven't any idea who wrote the epistle to the Hebrews, or why, other than what may be indicated in the letter itself. Does this mean that we can't understand it in any sense? I think not. We just have to recognize that information, which would assist the act of interpretation, is, in this case, missing.

Related to this warning is a second. For Protestants, scripture itself is authoritative. Our reconstructions, often highly conjectural of the historical circumstances under which a given biblical work was written and read, are not authoritative, by my understanding of Protestant theology. Those reconstructions may assist our understanding of the biblical text, but they are not, in and of themselves, of any religious authority.

Finally, we might add that the essential error of many exegetical theories is their exclusion of one or more of these three parties from consideration. While many important debates are continuing to influence interpretive theory, our evaluation of these debates would do well to retain a role for each of the three above-mentioned dimensions.

2. Formal and Dynamic Equivalence

One of the ongoing debates about translations revolves around the question of whether, and in what degree, the translation should reflect the syntax, or form, of the original language. All translators agree that the translation should reflect faithfully the message of the original, but all are not agreed on whether the translation should adhere closely to the grammatical forms of the original language.

Translations can be located on a spectrum, which would have, at one extreme, rigid adherence to the form of the original language (*formal equivalence*), and at the other extreme, complete disregard for the form (not the message) of the original language (*dynamic equivalence*). An interlinear would come the closest to the first extreme, followed by the New American Standard Bible (NASB). At the other extreme would be the New English Bible (NEB) and Transparent English Bible (TEV). In between would be the Revised Standard Version (RSV) and New International Version (NIV), with the RSV leaning more toward a formal equivalence, and the NIV leaning more toward a dynamic equivalence.

It is probably fair to say that most contemporary linguists favor the dynamic equivalence approach in theory, though they might be disappointed in the various attempts at producing one. The reason for preferring to reproduce the thought of the original without attempting to conform to its form is that all languages have their own syntax. While the syntax of one language may be similar to the syntax of other languages, it is also dissimilar as well. Thus, if we attempt to adhere to the formal syntax of another language, we reproduce forms which are abnormal or confusing, if not downright distracting in the target language.

For example, Greek tends to have very long sentences, whose various clauses are arranged in a logically hierarchical fashion. That is, there will be a number of dependent clauses connected to an independent clause. This type of sentence structure, perfectly normal in Greek, is called *hypotactic* (clauses are arranged logically under one another). English, by contrast, is not so comfortable with long sentences, and does not provide any easy way of indicating which clauses are dependent upon others. Our sentence structure is called *paratactic* (clauses are arranged logically alongside of one another). If we attempt to reproduce, in English, sentences of the same length as the

Greek original, our audience will not be able to follow our translation. Ephesians 1:3-14, for instance, is one sentence in Greek, with well-defined subordinate clauses. If we attempt to reproduce a sentence of this length in English, the result will be so awkward that few, if any, English readers would be able to follow it. Consequently, translators must break the longer Greek sentences into shorter English sentences.

For the pastor and teacher, it is important to be able to recognize the hypotactic structure of the original language, because it is frequently of theological and ethical significance. For instance, there is only one imperative (independent clause) in the Great Commission—"make disciples." All the other verbs are dependent. The other clauses help to describe what the commandment means. Most English translations, however, obscure this matter by translating the Great Commission as though it were a string of equivalent imperatives. What's worse, they tend to treat one of the dependent clauses as though it were the major (independent) clause ("Go"). So the teacher or pastor needs to be able to understand what is going on in the structure of the original language, without necessarily trying to reproduce it in an English translation.

There are other differences between the two languages. Greek typically uses passive verbs; English prefers active verbs. Greek typically makes nouns out of verbs (making "redemption" as common as "redeem"). Speakers of English are not as comfortable with these abstractions; we are happier with verbs. A dynamic equivalence translation will commonly reproduce the meaning of the Greek in a more natural manner in English. In 2 Thess 2:13, for instance, *pistei aletheias*, is translated "belief in the truth" (formal equivalence) by the RSV, but "the truth that you believe" (dynamic equivalence) by the NEB. The latter, while not any more accurate than the former, is a little more natural, and thus more easily understood.

A classic example of the difference between English and Greek syntax is evidenced by the difference in their respective employment of the participle. First, the Greek participle is much more common than the English. But the Greek participle is also used differently than the English participle. Greek commonly employs the participle in an attributive fashion, as a verbal adjective. This is very rare in English. James Taylor does sing about the "The Walking Man," but this is rare outside of artistic expression. We would normally produce a relative clause, "the man who walks." Because of the differences in the way the two languages use their respective participles, we simply cannot translate a Greek participle with an English participle in many cases, without being obscure or ambiguous. *Dikaiothentes* in Romans 5:1 should not be translated, "having been justified" (NASB: formal equivalence), but, "since we are justified" (RSV: dynamic equivalence).

There are problems, however, with dynamic equivalence translations. Since the translator is "freer" from the grammatical forms of the original language he is more likely to exceed the bounds of an accurate translation, in an effort to speak naturally in the native language. That is, the dynamic equivalence translations are capable of being more natural and more precise than are formal equivalence translations, but they are also more capable of being *precisely wrong*. For instance, in Romans 8:3, Paul uses the phrase: *dia tes sarkos*. A formal equivalent translation, the RSV, renders this "by the flesh," which is faithful to the original but somewhat ambiguous in

English. The NIV renders this much more precisely, by the phrase, "by the sinful nature." Unfortunately, the NIV is precisely *wrong* here, because Paul is not talking about a lower nature, or a sinful nature at all. In fact, he is not speaking anthropologically, but redemptive-historically. In this particular case, I believe we would be better off with the ambiguous "flesh," and have to ask what 'flesh' means for Paul, than to have the more precise but utterly un-Pauline "sinful nature."

Another problem associated with dynamic equivalence translations is related to their use as study Bibles. Since a given word may have a number of meanings, it is frequently impossible, and more frequently confusing, to attempt to translate a given Greek word with the same English word in every case. Consequently, the dynamic equivalence translation can give a more specific rendering in English, being unbound by an attempt to reproduce the same Greek word in the same English manner. This produces better understanding, frequently, of individual sentences or clauses. However, it does not permit the English reader to know when the same Greek word lay behind two different English words. Since the only way to know what a word means is by first examining its full range of uses, there is no way for the English reader to know what words are behind the English words found.

For instance, when Paul says he could not address the Corinthians as *pneumatikoi*, but rather as *sarkinoi* (1 Cor 3), he employs the adjectival forms of what we normally translate "Spirit" and "flesh." And, in Romans 8 (as well as elsewhere), it is clear that life in the Spirit is redeemed life; whereas life in the flesh is unredeemed life. If the adjectives in 1 Cor are translated "spiritual," and "fleshly," the reader can see the correspondence to other Pauline passages, and understand that Paul is saying, in effect, "I could not address you as redeemed people, but as unredeemed people." But the NIV construes *sarx* as "sinful nature" in Rom 8, and *sarkinos* as "worldly" in 1 Cor 3, with the result that the reader of this translation is not aware that in the original the same root form was employed. The conclusion of this is that the dynamic equivalence translation, when done well, renders in more precise and more vivid English particular expressions. However, it makes it more difficult to compare individual passages with parallel passages elsewhere.

In any given congregation, a variety of translations will be present. The teachers in the church must have the competence to discern which one represents the original most accurately in English in any circumstance. In my judgment, none of the contemporary translations is manifestly superior to the others. Each is a blend of strengths and weaknesses, due to the difficulty of the task.

From the pulpit, of course, some versions can be excluded rather easily. Paraphrases, while useful to illustrate a point, should never be used as the basic sermon text, because they reflect so thoroughly the opinions of the paraphraser. Also, children's Bibles, such as the Good News, and, to a lesser degree, the NIV should not be used as the basis of a sermon directed toward the entire congregation. The NASB should not be used, simply because its English is atrocious. Its rigid adherence to the formal equivalence principle, while making it highly useful in the study, renders it completely inappropriate in a setting where communication is important.

The NIV should not be used from the pulpit, in my judgment, because it is a sectarian translation. It is a self-confessedly "evangelical" translation, which excluded non-evangelicals from the translation process. It is therefore ecclesiastically unacceptable (it excludes from the outset people who don't call themselves "evangelical," just as the *Kingdom Translation* excludes people who don't call themselves Jehovah's Witnesses). In fact, even for study purposes, one will have to be cautious about the evangelical bias reflected in this translation, whereby the weaknesses, as well as the strengths, of evangelicalism have not been offset by a more "inclusive" committee.

Specifically, the NIV shows many signs of being individualistic, experientialist, and revivalistic (I am speaking about the NIV New Testament; I haven't evaluated the NIV Old Testament thoroughly yet). At the same time, the NIV ought to be in the minister's study because it is a good illustration of the demands of a dynamic equivalence translation, and it is also very successful at many points. The RSV, reflecting the breadth of the church, a high style of English, and a reasonably accurate representation of the original text, is perhaps the preferred text for pulpit use.

3. Translation is a theological task

It has become increasingly clear that translation cannot really be performed in a theological vacuum. When a variety of linguistic options present themselves, theological factors can influence the decision to choose one option over the other. In fact, such factors should influence the translation. The resolution of the translation question about how to translate

86

telos in Romans 10:4 is resolved in large part by resolving larger questions about Paul's theology; how he understands the relation between the older testament and the Christ event, etc. Since theology is to be determined by the Bible, and since translating the Bible is determined, at least in part, by theological considerations, it is easy to see that there is something of a circle here. Fortunately, it is not a vicious cycle, because if one is willing to entertain sympathetically a variety of options, one can grow in the confidence with which one evaluates a given translation. One must never pretend, however, that translation is a step of "pre-exegesis" or "pre-interpretation." The first step of interpretation is translation. This step will influence all other steps, so it must be approached with the entire arsenal of theological tools.

Semantic Theory

It is appropriate now to move to some consideration of dealing with the meaning of individual words (commonly called lexical semantics). A lexicon in the hands of an over-imaginative preacher may be the deadliest of all human instruments. In terms of sheer percentages, more pulpit nonsense may be attributable to a misunderstanding of how words communicate meaning than any other interpretive error. Since the technical study of linguistics began in the early nineteenth century, a number of very valuable insights have been discovered by the linguists. What follows is an attempt at providing some of their most useful insights for those who want to teach and preach faithfully.

1. Semantic Field and Context

Most words can mean a number of things. Take the English word, "run." It can appear in the following (and many more) contexts:

> The athlete is running.
> Her nose is running.
> We scored a run in the sixth inning.
> I have a run in my stocking.
> Does your car run?
> My computer runs on Windows.
> For how long is the movie running?
> You want to run that by me again?
> His sermons seem to run on forever.
> She's running the flag up the pole.
> Jackson is running for President.
> Who left the water running?

Enough, already. It is obvious that most words can mean a number of different things. How do we know what a word means in a given circumstance? Well, we don't just choose the one we prefer. In fact, there are two components to meaning: semantic field and semantic context.

By semantic field, we mean the full range of ways the word has and can be used (an example is the above, partial semantic field for "run"). By examining the "field" of possible meanings, we begin to narrow the options. Normally, there are still too many options, so we have to take another step. The second step is to determine the semantic context. If "run," for instance, can refer to rapid, bipedal locomotion in some contexts, we can eliminate that option in contexts where there are no legs or feet. If "run" can mean "flow," or "drip," it is a possible way of understanding it where noses and faucets appear, but not where liquids do not appear. In everyday speech, we do this kind of comparison to semantic context so rapidly and unreflectively that we are not normally aware of doing it. But we do it nevertheless, and normally with great accuracy. It is imperative that we do this with biblical literature as well. No word brings its full semantic field with it into any given context. Yet many fanciful pulpit statements are due to the attempt to do this very thing.

2. "Root" Meanings

Many people speak of "root meanings." Many people speak of ghosts. Neither exists. Apparently, when people speak of "root" meanings of words, they are attempting to find the distilled essence, or the common semantic range of the word in each of its contexts. This may, by dumb luck, work in some circumstances, but it won't work in most. What common "root" meaning is there in the word "run" which can account for the variety of uses listed above? Is it motion? Perhaps, for the athlete, the flag, even the nose (which doesn't move itself, but its contents do). But is there any "motion" involved in the statement that a person is running for an office? Is any motion taking place when a movie "runs" for six weeks? Is a "run" in a stocking a movement of some sort? I fail to see how there is, without redefining the word "motion" to include virtually everything. And if we do this, then we aren't learning anything specific about the term in question (This is the practical deficiency of the Componential Analysis approach to Semantics; if one finds an element common enough to be related to all the various uses, it isn't specific enough to be any real help in any given context). In actual fact, we don't really know why people use terms in such a broad range of ways as they do. But the answer certainly doesn't lie in the fact of some alleged "root" meaning, common to all uses. Thus, for interpretation's sake, it is better not to speak of "root" meanings at all. Just look at the entire semantic field, and then limit that field by the contextual considerations.

This doesn't mean that there are no similarities in the variety of a term's uses. If we return to "run," we can determine several "sub"-fields. We can see "run" used of liquids, to indicate they are flowing. We can see "run" used with machines to indicate that they are operating as they should. We can see it used in reference to putting one foot ahead of another repeatedly, in rapid succession, which would embrace the athlete, and, by extension, the "runs" in a baseball game (which are a short-hand reference to someone "running" around the bases). But these fields do not appear to be related to each other, and worse, these fields do not account for the stocking or the flag. Perhaps we ought to just bring "root" meanings out once a year, on October 31st, and then put them back for the rest of the year.

3. Etymologies and Semantic Change

Etymology is a perfectly valid field of study. Etymology is the study of the history of a word's usage. It has the historical benefit of demonstrating to us what a word might have meant in a given period. One thing etymologists have discovered, of course, is that words change over time. That is, people apparently use terms in an increasing variety of ways, extending known usages, and coining new usages. Thus, the history of a word's usage is not necessarily any help in determining its meaning in a particular context. And certainly, it is not the case that the "earliest" known meaning is the "true," "real," or, need

I say it, "root" meaning. "Gay," for instance, might well have meant "happy" or "carefree" in certain places in certain times. It most emphatically does not mean that today in San Francisco. Do not be misled; a "happy" hour at a "gay" bar may be a very miserable experience for a heterosexual teetotaler.

The biblical interpreter is not particularly interested in what a term may have meant several centuries prior to the time in question. Rather, the biblical interpreter wants to know what range of meaning a term had in the period in question. Etymology is not particularly helpful as a guide to the meaning of a term in any given context. Semantic context is the more reliable guide.

4. Polyvalency

You may run across (oops, another use of "run") this term from time to time, so you may as well know what it means. "Polyvalency" refers to the ability of a given term to have a number of meanings in any given historical period. "Run" is polyvalent. It is important for the interpreter to be aware of the full range of possible meanings of a given word, before determining what it means in its given context.

5. Words and Concepts

For the sake of clarity, it is helpful to distinguish between a word and a concept. Most words can be employed to denote a number of concepts, and most concepts can be addressed by using a range of terms. Thus, *charis* is a word; *grace* is a concept which can be labeled in a variety of ways. So, if you want to study, "The Grace of God in the New Testament," you would certainly include not only a word study of *charis*, but also passages which refer to God's gracious activity without employing that particular term. For instance, the parable of the laborers in the vineyard reflects God's gracious character, as those who come along late in the day receive equal recompense with those who have labored all day. God graciously gives the kingdom not only to the Jews, but also to the Gentiles, who come on the scene a bit late, redemptive-historically speaking.

6. Semantic "Minimalism"

One of the best axioms to apply when attempting to discover the meaning of any given word was first coined by Ferdinand de Saussure and his followers. The best meaning of a given term is the meaning which *contributes the least to the overall meaning* of the sentence. In most communication acts, we do not "load up" a given word with a lot of meaning. Rather, we speak in paragraphs and—the individual words have little meaning in and of themselves, but much meaning when tied to one another. Many seminarians and preachers seem to be unaware of this, for they frequently interpret the Bible as though its individual words were almost magical, possessing great truths and that in six or seven letters. There are very few technical terms in any language, which are more heavily "loaded" than most words.

Concluding Observations

If one were to state briefly the results of linguistic study in the last few generations, one would certainly have to refer to the importance of context. Linguistics has made us repeatedly aware of the fact that the fundamental communicative unit is the sentence, not the word. Individual words, removed from the context of a sentence, rarely communicate effectively. Words strung together, mutually supporting and interpreting one another, can communicate very effectively. For biblical students, this means that we must look at the larger units of communication (the sentence and paragraph) at least as seriously as we look at individual words. We must be aware of the fact that a given word can signify a number of different things in a number of different contexts.

Personally, I would like to see more sermons on whole chapters of scripture, and even on entire books, and fewer sermons on a verse here or there. If a person can produce a single 20-minute distillation of Romans 1-11, he can certainly handle Romans 6:3 when it shows up. If the contextual emphasis of contemporary linguistics can help us see the "forest" of a biblical book, as opposed to merely the "trees" of individual words, it will have done us and God's kingdom a great service.

Appendix D:

A GUIDE TO MODERN VERSIONS OF THE BIBLE

New King James Version • New American Standard Bible • English Standard Version • Revised Standard Version • New International Version • New Living Translation • New English Bible

By Dr. Herbert Samworth
(http://www.solagroup.org/articles/historyofthebible/hotb_0003. html)

If you had been looking to purchase a Bible fifty years ago, your choices would have been between the King James Version and one or two others. However, today you are faced with shelves and shelves of Bibles that command their own section in your local Christian bookstore. It is easy to be overwhelmed by the sheer number of available options. Which one should you acquire? What factors should be taken into consideration before making your decision?

We will look at a short list of seven of the most popular versions of the Bible that are available today. But why these seven? First, these versions, with one exception, include only translations that use the most current versions of the Hebrew and Greek texts as the bases for the translations. Second, the translation work on the Bibles listed has been done by a committee, not by just one person. Experience has demonstrated that in a multitude of translators, as well as counselors, there is wisdom. Third, we must also state that only translations have been selected for inclusion. Paraphrases of the Scriptures have increased in popularity in recent years, but they tend to be the work of an individual. Finally, all of the versions and translations that will be noted are for Protestants and Evangelicals. While there has been an increase in English translations for Roman Catholics, they have not been included in this list.

Methods of translation

Before we look at the various versions, a reminder is needed concerning how the translation of the Bible is done. The translator of God's Word has an awesome responsibility. On the one hand, there is the concern to be faithful to the original source languages. The Scriptures were originally given in Hebrew, Aramaic, and Greek. This necessitates a thorough knowledge of the original language in both its culture and context. In addition, in the case of the Scriptures, there is an additional difficulty because there is both a chronological and cultural gap between the world of the Bible and the world of the twenty-first century.

The translator also has the responsibility to communicate meaningfully the author's message to the reader in the reader's culture and context. Therefore, the translator must be skillful in the understanding of the receptor language and be acquainted with his audience.

If the items noted above were the only obstacles, the task would be daunting in itself. However, we must add another factor to the translation process. That is the factor of the theory or method used in the translation. There are two basic theories of translation although there may be a great amount of overlap between them.

The first is known as the **formal** or **verbal equivalence** translation theory. In this method, the translator selects a word in the receptor language that is the equivalent to the one found in the source language. If this principle is applied in a slavish manner it can result in an awkward literalistic translation. However, if done in order to assure meaningful communication, the result is a translation that effectively communicates the original sense of the source language.

The second translation theory is called the **functional** or **dynamic equivalence** method. The translator attempts to reproduce in the receptor language the thoughts and ideas of the source language in equivalent concepts. While this may result in meaningful communication, there is the danger of distorting the meaning or sense of the source language. It is important to state that the two theories of translation are rarely accomplished perfectly. However, one or the other will predominate in the translation.

The list

The **NEW KING JAMES VERSION:** This is the only translation that does not use the latest critical editions of the Greek and Hebrew texts. The Textus Receptus remains the primary textual base of this translation. Perhaps some of the history of this King James Version, also known as the "Authorized Version," will be helpful to the reader.

What is the Textus Receptus?

The Textus Receptus (TR), or "Received Text," is the term used to refer to the first printed editions of the Greek New Testament as they appeared from 1516-1633. Most prominent

96

of these publications are editions by Erasmus, Robert Stephanus, Theodore Beza, and the Elzevir brothers. These editions all drew from a mix of available Greek manuscripts and became the text basis of the Bible for centuries. But throughout the nineteenth century, scores of manuscripts, dated earlier than those used by the TR scholars, were coming to light, and the age of the "critical text" had begun. By 1882 the Wescott-Hort Greek New Testament had supplanted the TR as the standard edition of the Greek text.

There is no doubt that until recently the dominant version of the Bible in the English language has been the King James Version. Originally printed in 1611, it has undergone several revisions, although minor, during its history. It has been praised for the majesty of its language and beauty of expression. However, with newly discovered editions of the Greek texts and subsequent translations, the King James Version began to decline in popularity. Changes have taken place in the English language that rendered the Shakespearian language and cadence of the King James outdated. Complaints were voiced that its language was unintelligible to an increasing number of people.

However, among certain groups the King James Version has retained its popularity. Some have gone so far as to adopt what has been called a "King James only" mentality. Thus, the King James Version is not only considered to be the best translation of the Scriptures but the only acceptable one. This position has escalated to the point where there are some who believe that the translation of the King James Version was providentially guided by the Holy Spirit and the translation is without error. Even the original texts of the Hebrew and Greek can be corrected by it. Although this is an extreme position, many people, especially of the older generations, are convinced that no other version is worthy to dislodge the King James Version from its dominant position.

In an attempt to safeguard the position of the King James, Thomas Nelson published what is called the New King James Version. The translators of the New King James emphasized their concern to continue the same tradition as the King James Version. However, the translators have updated the English in a more contemporary manner while seeking to preserve "for today's readers the spiritual treasures found especially in the Authorized Version of the Holy Scriptures."

The New King James Bible would be a good choice for someone who is looking to retain the elevation of language and diction found in the original Authorized Version.

All the remaining versions surveyed use the critical editions of the Greek New Testament and the Hebrew Text. We will note them in a spectrum, beginning with those that use the formal translation theory to those that are translated using the dynamic equivalence theory.

The **NEW AMERICAN STANDARD BIBLE** has received high marks for its fidelity to the original meaning of the original text while being criticized for its cumbersome English. This version can be traced back to the first translation made from the Westcott and Hort text in 1881-85. This translation was called the English Revised Version and was printed in 1885. The translation committee included members from England and the United States. The American committee disagreed with a number of choices selected by the British committee but agreed not to publish them for sixteen years. In 1901, the American Standard Version (ASV) was published which included the changes made by the American committee. It proved to be an accurate, albeit literal and somewhat cumbersome, translation. In the 1960s an updating of this version was undertaken by the Lockman Foundation which holds the copyright. The Foundation was distressed that the use of the American Standard Version was "fast decreasing from the scene." In the words of the Lockman Foundation, they felt "an urgency to rescue this noble achievement from an inevitable demise, to preserve it as a heritage for coming generations, and to do so in such a form as the demands of passing time dictate."

The New American Standard New Testament was published in 1963 and the entire Bible in 1971. The NASB continues the rigid verbal equivalence translation as found in the ASV. In its favor it can be stated that it reflects the wording of the original languages and is a good version for Bible study. However, it also shows the defects of the ASV in that it is not as readable for devotional and worship purposes. Later editions of the NASB have sought to correct its wooden style by removing archaic words and improving its vocabulary and style.

The **ENGLISH STANDARD VERSION** is the latest translation to be issued from the press. It is too early to tell if it will be successful but initial sales have been very encouraging. The ESV claims to be "an essentially literal translation, emphasizing word-for-word precision." Thus, it is to be considered a formal translation. The ESV also has an interesting history. It is an updating of the Revised Standard Version (see below). The Revised Standard Version has never been accepted by the evangelical community because of its association with the World Council of Churches and translations that appear to deny the virgin birth of Christ. While the RSV has not been popular among Evangelicals in the United States, it has been received with a greater appreciation in England.

The strength of the English Standard Version is its combination of formal adherence to the text of Scripture and beauty of language. It is also in a position to benefit from the controversy surrounding the gender inclusive policies being followed by Today's New International Version. In addition, there appears to be a waning of interest in the functional or dynamic equivalence theory of translation. If one is looking for a balanced combination of scholarship in translation and fluency of language, one might consider this version.

The parent to the English Standard Version was the **REVISED STANDARD VERSION**. First published in 1946 in the New Testament and 1952 in the Old Testament, it has received mixed reviews. Several unfortunate translations of key verses have tainted it with charges of liberalism and the fact that the copyright is owned by the National Council of Churches has reinforced the negative image. This is rather unfortunate because, on balance, the version is an admirable attempt to balance fidelity of translation in a formal manner and beauty of language.

The Revised Standard Version has been updated to include changes in the text base and to update language. This version has also received criticism for its inclusion of the Apocrypha that makes it more acceptable in ecumenical circles and gender inclusive language. Despite these criticisms, many are convinced that this version is the most up to date in biblical scholarship.

The fifth version of the Bible that we wish to consider is the **NEW INTERNATIONAL VERSION**. This Bible and the two that follow are translated according to the functional or dynamic equivalence theory.

The New International Version project was undertaken because of dissatisfaction with the Revised Standard Version. A committee was formed in 1963 to prepare a new translation for the conservative/evangelical community. Additional support for this translation came from the International Bible Society and the Zondervan Publishing House.

The New Testament was printed in 1973 and the Old Testament followed in 1978. As stated above this translation was done in the dynamic equivalence method and this limits its use for Biblical study and word analysis. None of this has hindered its acceptance because the New International Version has become a best seller and is the most popular version today both in evangelical and the larger Christian circles.

Controversy has dogged this translation, however. Several years ago, there were plans to produce a gender-neutral edition of the NIV. Strong conservative pressure prevented these plans from going forward and an agreement to cancel the edition was signed by both parties. However, within the last several months, this agreement was formally disavowed by the International Bible Society and an edition called Today's New International Version (TNIV) was announced. This edition will use "inclusive language." The announcement raised an outburst from the conservatives who also were parties to the original agreement. As of this date the controversy continues and whether or not this edition comes to the market remains to be seen.

The plans to produce this version have opened again the whole question of Bible translation and the correct manner of doing it. While it is regrettable that this issue has divided many evangelicals, there is the real possibility that the long-term effect will be for good because Bible translation theory, the implied catering to contemporary and cultural pressures, and the marketing of various versions that are part of Bible production will now be examined with greater scrutiny. Hopefully, this will result in a greater emphasis being placed on the importance of a translation that is both faithful to the text in all areas and its readability. However, a good translation must also lead further to the reading, studying and application of the Scriptures to the life of the individual.

Another version that has captured the attention of the Evangelical community is called the **NEW LIVING TRANSLATION**. This version also has an interesting history. In the early 1970s, Kenneth Taylor of Tyndale Publishing House produced a paraphrase known as the Living Bible. This attempt was to make the Scriptures as meaningful in the modern English idiom as possible to the general reader from a position of rigid orthodoxy.

The commercial success of the Living Bible was overwhelming and it became very popular among Evangelicals despite its limitations as to coherence with the original text. In the mid-1990s a decision was made to update the Living Bible. A translation team was assembled to rework the translation and modify it from a paraphrase to a dynamic equivalence translation. The language was also improved to make it more accurate and readable. This is the first case where a paraphrase was modified to become a dynamic equivalence translation. The New Living Translation has been marketed extensively and has proven to be popular among Evangelicals.

The final version that we will note is called the **NEW ENGLISH BIBLE**. This version was originally conceived in the late 1940s. It was one of the first British attempts at a dynamic equivalence translation and was well accepted in England because of its attempt to retain formal and traditional English vocabulary and diction. However, its popularity with British readers was not matched by readers from other countries due to its British character.

This version, like many of the others we have noted, has also been updated to remove some of its limitations and to improve its style. It has never been popular in the United States and the reader may encounter some difficulty in locating a copy.

TRANSLATION COMPARISON
Romans 3:23-26

NKJV	NASB	ESV	RSV	NIV	NLT	NEB
For all have sinned and fall short of the glory of God,	For all have sinned and fall short of the glory of God,	For all have sinned and fall short of the glory of God,	Since all have sinned and fall short of the glory of God,	For all have sinned and fall short of the glory of God,	For all have sinned; all fall short of God's glorious standard.	For all alike have sinned, and are deprived of the divine splendour,
being justified freely by His grace through the redemption that is in Christ Jesus,	being justified as a gift by His grace through the redemption which is in Christ Jesus;	and are justified by his grace as a gift, through the redemption that is in Christ Jesus,	they are justified by his grace as a gift, through the redemption which is in Christ Jesus,	and are justified freely by his grace through the redemption that came by Christ Jesus.	Yet now God in his gracious kindness declares us not guilty. He has done this through Christ Jesus, who has freed us by taking away our sins.	and all are justified by God's free grace alone, through his act of liberation in the Person of Christ Jesus.
whom God set forth to be a propitiation by His blood, through faith, to demonstrate His righteousness, because in His forbearance God had passed over the sins that were	whom God displayed publicly as a propitiation in His blood through faith. This was to demonstrate His righteousness, because in the forbearance of God He passed over the sins	whom God put forward as a propitiation by his blood, to be received by faith. This was to show God's righteousness, because in his divine forbearance he had	whom God put forward as an expiation by his blood, to be received by faith. This was to show God's righteousness, because in his divine forbearance he had passed over former sins;	God presented him as a sacrifice of atonement, through faith in his blood. He did this to demonstrate his justice, because in his forbearance he had left the sins committed	For God sent Jesus to take the punishment for our sins and to satisfy God's anger against us. We are made right with God when we believe that Jesus shed his	For God designed him to be the means of expiating sin by his sacrificial death, effective through faith. God meant by this to demonstrate his justice, because in his

104

previously committed,	previously committed;	passed over former sins.		beforehand unpunished;	blood, sacrificing his life for us. God was being entirely fair and just when he did not punish those who sinned in former times.	forbearance he had overlooked the sins of the past-
to demonstrate at the present time His righteousness, that He might be just and the justifier of the one who has faith in Jesus.	for the demonstration, I say, of His righteousness at the present time, that He might be just and the justifier of the one who has faith in Jesus.	It was to show his righteousness at the present time, so that he might be just and the justifier of the one who has faith in Jesus.	it was to prove at the present time that he himself is righteous and that he justifies him who has faith in Jesus.	he did it to demonstrate his justice at the present time, so as to be just and the one who justifies those who have faith in Jesus.	And he is entirely fair and just in this present time when he declares sinners to be right in his sight because they believe in Jesus.	to demonstrate his justice now in the present, showing that he is himself just and also justifies any man who puts his faith in Jesus.

Conclusion

On the one hand, there is reason to lament the proliferation of versions because the reason for the new translations appears to be market driven. On the other hand, there is reason for thankfulness that the Word of God is available to us in so many versions.

However, we must understand two things. First, we must keep in mind that the Bible must be prayed over, studied, and committed to the heart in order for it to function in the manner that God intended. The truth of Scripture is given to us for living. We may own every version of the Scriptures that is available and not be profited one bit. We must be doers of the Word. Debates can be multiplied regarding the correct way to translate the Bible. It certainly is a topic that merits serious consideration. But it is the power of the Word of God that effects the changes in thinking and doing that are so critical today.

In the second place, we must remember there remain countless peoples in the world today who have never owned or even seen a copy of the Scriptures. Gratitude should flow from our hearts to God for the privilege of having the Word of God in our own language. However, in addition to gratitude, there must be the determination to make the Word of God available to all the peoples of the world in a language they can understand.

Appendix E

THE EXEGETICAL PROCESS

From: https://www.google.mw/the+exegetical+process&
newwindow=1&source=lnms&tbm=isch&sa

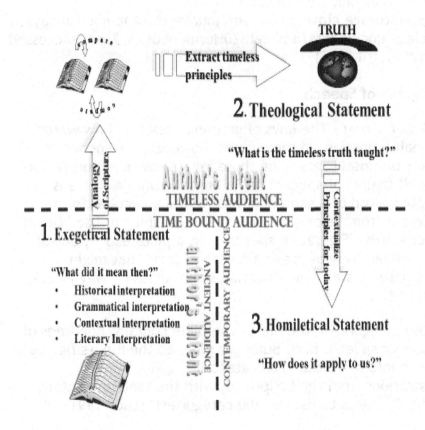

Appendix F

INTERPRETING FIGURES OF SPEECH

Mike Vlach, Hermeneutics: Principles of Bible Interpretation: Part 2 of 2, Indian Hills Community Church Center for Biblical Studies, Lincoln, www.ihcc.org. http://storage.cloversites.com/journeythruthebiblesundaysch oolclass/documents/Biblical%20Hermeneutics_2.pdf. Accessed on 12th April 2015)

I. Figures of Speech

A. **A definition** - The laws of grammar describe how words normally function. In some cases, however, the speaker or writer purposely sets aside those laws to use new forms, forms we call figures of speech. As Bullinger wrote, 'A figure is simply a word or a sentence thrown into a peculiar form, different from its original or simplest meaning or use.' Or, in other words, "Figurative speech ... is a picturesque, out-of-the-ordinary way of presenting literal facts that might otherwise be stated in a normal, plain, ordinary way" (Zuck 1991, 147).

B. Use of figures in the Bible "The Bible contains hundreds of figures of speech. E.W. Bullinger grouped the Bible's figures of speech into more than 200 categories, giving 8,000 illustrations from the Scriptures, with the table of contents taking 28 pages to list the 200 categories!" (Zuck 1991, 143).

C. EXAMPLES
- Ex. If we say "It is raining hard," we are using a normal, plain statement. But if we say, "It is raining cats and dogs," we have used a sentence that means the same thing but is an unusual, more colorful way of expressing the same thought.
- Ex. Calling someone who deceives others "a snake."

- Ex. Calling your companion "Sweetheart" or "Honey."
- Ex. "Get off your high horse."
- Ex. A long pass in football is "a bomb."
- Ex. "Chicago Bulls"
- Ex. "He's flipped his lid."
- Ex. "She has a green thumb."
- Biblical ex. Jesus is "the lamb of God" (John 1:29).

D. Why use figures of speech? (Zuck 1991, 144-45)

Figurative speech ... is a picturesque, out-of-the-ordinary way of presenting literal facts that might otherwise be stated in a normal, plain, ordinary way.

- Adds color and vividness "To say, 'The Lord is my rock' (Ps. 18:2) is a colorful, vivid way of saying the Lord is One on whom I can depend because He is strong and unmovable" (Zuck 1991, 144). Figures of speech express truths in vivid and interesting ways.
- Attracts Attention "A listener or reader immediately perks up because of the uniqueness of figures of speech. This is evident when Paul wrote, "Watch out for those dogs" (Phil. 3:2), or when James wrote, 'The tongue is a fire' (James 3:6). When a comparison is made between two things that are normally not alike or normally not compared, then surprise occurs" (Zuck 1991, 144-45).
- Makes the abstract more concrete "Underneath are the everlasting arms" (Deut. 33:27) is certainly more concrete than the statement, 'The Lord will take care of you and support you.'" (Zuck 1991, 145)
- Aids in retention "Hosea's statement, 'The Israelites are ... like a stubborn heifer' (Hosea 4:16), is more easily remembered than if Hosea had written, 'Israel is terribly stubborn' ... Figures of speech are used in many languages because they are easily remembered and make indelible impressions" (Zuck 1991. 145).

- Abbreviates an idea "They capture and convey the idea in a brief way. Because they are graphic, they eliminate the need for elaborate description. They say a lot in a little. The well-known metaphor, 'The Lord is my Shepherd' (Ps. 23:1), conveys briefly many ideas about the Lord's relationship to His own" (Zuck 1991, 145).

E. Figures of speech consistent with the literal method of interpretation It must be remembered that figures of speech convey literal truths and, therefore, do not argue against a literal interpretation of the Bible. Behind every figure of speech is a literal meaning, and by means of the historical-grammatical exegesis of the text, these literal meanings are to be sought out. To argue for a mystical, allegorical or spiritualizing method to interpreting Scripture based on figures of speech is fallacious. "Figurative language then is not antithetical to literal interpretation; it is a part of it. Perhaps it is better not to speak of 'figurative versus literal' interpretation, but of 'ordinary-literal' versus 'figurative-literal' interpretation" (Zuck 1991, 147).
- Ex. Herod a fox Jesus, in calling Herod a "fox," (Luke 13:32) could have said, "Herod is sly and cunning." But by using "fox" He conveyed the same literal truth in more vivid terms.
- Ex. Revelation Many want to spiritualize the book of Revelation and other portions of Scripture because of the many symbols used. But, even in apocalyptic literature, each symbol conveys a literal truth.

II. Examples of figures of speech

A. Simile – "A simile is a comparison in which one thing explicitly (by using like or as) resembles another" (Zuck 1991, 148).
1. Ex. "All men are like grass" (1 Pet. 1:24).
2. Ex. "And he will be like a tree ..." (Psalm 1:3).
3. Ex. "And his feet were like burnished bronze" (Rev. 1:15).

B. Metaphor – "A comparison in which one thing is, acts like, or represents another (in which the two are basically unalike). In a metaphor the comparison is implicit, whereas in a simile it is explicit. A clue to identifying a metaphor is that the verb will always be in the form of "to be" ("is," "are," "were," "have been")" (Zuck 1991, 149).
  1. Ex. "All flesh is grass" (Isa. 40:6, KJV).
  2. Ex. "You are the light of the world" (Matt. 5:14).

Anthropomorphism—The attributing of human features or actions to God.

C. Hypocatastasis - A comparison in which the likeness is implied by a direct naming.
  1. Ex. "Dogs have surrounded me" (Ps. 22:16).
  2. Ex. "Look, the Lamb of God" (John 1:29).

D. Personification- The ascribing of human characteristics or actions to inanimate objects or ideas or to animals.
  • Ex. "The moon will be abashed and the sun ashamed" (Isa. 24:23).
  • Ex. "And all the trees of the field will clap their hands" (Isa. 55:12).

E. Anthropomorphism - The attributing of human features or actions to God.
  1. Ex. God's fingers (Ps. 8:3)
  2. Ex. God's ear (Ps. 31:2)
  3. Ex. God's eyes (2 Chron. 16:9)
  4. Ex. "So the Lord changed His mind ...." (Exodus 32:14).

F. Apostrophe - "Addressing a thing as if it were a person, or an absent or imaginary person as if he were present" (Hendricks 1991, 266).
  1. Ex. "O death, where is your victory?" (1 Cor. 15:55).
  2. Ex. "Listen, O Earth, and all who are in it" (Micah 1:2).

G. Hyperbole - "A hyperbole is a deliberate exaggeration, in which more is said than is literally meant, in order to add emphasis" (Zuck 1991, 154). A common example: "I told him a thousand times to clean up his room."

1. Ex. "The cities are large and fortified to heaven" (Deut. 1:28).
2. Ex. "Every night I make my bed swim, I dissolve my couch with my tears" (Ps. 6:6).
3. Ex. David said of Saul and Jonathan after their deaths, "They were swifter than eagles, they were stronger than lions" (2 Sam. 1:23)

H. Euphemism - This is the substituting of an inoffensive or mild expression for an offensive or personal one. In English, we speak euphemistically of death by saying that a person "passed on," or 'went home.' For example, the Bible refers to death for the believer as a falling asleep (Acts 7:60; 1 Thess. 4:13-15).

III. Interpreting Figures of Speech "Generally an expression is figurative when it is out of character with the subject discussed, or is contrary to fact, experience, or observation" (Zuck 1991, 145).

A. Use the literal sense unless there is some good reason not to "If the literal sense makes common sense, seek no other sense." For example, "When John wrote that 144,000 will be sealed, with 12,000 from each of the 12 tribes of Israel, there is no reason not to take those numbers in their normal, literal sense (see Rev. 7:4-8). And yet in the following verse John referred to "the Lamb" (v.9), clearly a reference to Jesus Christ, not an animal, as indicated by John 1:29" (Zuck 1991, 146).

B. Use the figurative sense when the passage indicates doing so "Some passages tell you up front that they involve figurative imagery. For instance, whenever you come across a dream or a vision, you can expect to find symbolic language because that's the language of dreams" (Hendricks 1991, 260) (Exs. Daniel 2, 7, 8, 11; Ezek. 1; Revelation).

C. Use the figurative sense if a literal meaning is impossible or absurd "This is where we need some sanctified common sense. God does not shroud Himself in unknowable mysticism. When He wants to tell us something, He tells us. He doesn't confound us with nonsense. However, He often used symbolism to make His points. Yet He expects us to read them as symbols, not absurdities" (Hendricks, p. 261). Examples include, the Lord having wings (Ps. 57:1) or trees clapping their hands (Isa. 55:12).

D. Use the figurative sense if a literal meaning would involve something immoral. For example, since it would be cannibalistic to eat the flesh of Jesus and to drink His blood, He obviously was speaking figuratively (John 6:53-58).

E. Use the figurative sense if the expression is an obvious figure of speech. The biblical text often signals its use of figures of speech by terms such as "like" or "as" For example, "Like a gold ring in a pig's snout is a beautiful woman who shows no discretion" (Prov. 11:22).

Interpreting Parables

I. Introduction to Parables

A. Where does the term "parable" come from? The Greek word is a compound of two words, para (beside) and ballo (to throw or cast). The idea, then, is that facts in one realm which the hearers know are cast alongside facts in the spiritual realm so that they will see, by analogy or correspondence, what is true in this realm.

B. Definition: A parable is a true-to-life story that illustrates a spiritual truth. "Thus, a parable is something placed alongside something else for the purpose of comparison. The typical parable uses a common event of natural life to emphasize or clarify an important spiritual truth" (Virkler 1981, 162-63).

C. Used by Jesus "Jesus, the master teacher, used parables regularly as He taught. The Greek word for parable occurs nearly fifty times in the synoptic gospels in connection with His ministry, suggesting that parables were one of His favorite teaching devices" (Virkler 1981, 163).

D. Purpose of parables
- To conceal truth from those who would not believe (Matt. 13:10-12)
- To reveal truth to believers (Matt. 13:10-12) "While these purposes may seem contradictory, the answer to this dilemma may lay in the nature of the hearers. Since the teachers of the Law had already demonstrated their unbelief and rejection of Jesus, they revealed the hardened condition of their hearts. This made them unable to comprehend the meaning of His parables. Blinded by unbelief, they rejected Him, and so as He spoke in parables they normally would not comprehend their meaning. On the other hand, His followers, open to Him and His truths, would understand the parables." (Zuck 1991, 197) "It may be that as a man resists truth and yields to sin, he becomes less and less able to understand spiritual truth. Thus, the same parables that brought insight to faithful believers were without meaning to those who were hardening their hearts against the truth" (Virkler 1981, 164-65).
- To give new truth concerning the Kingdom "If Bible students do not recognize the emphasis on the kingdom in the parables, they overlook an important key to understanding those stories and why Jesus told them" (Zuck 1991, 211).

114

II. Guidelines for interpreting parables

A. Note the story's natural meaning "To understand the spiritual truth properly, it is essential first to comprehend fully the true-to-life incident ... As you understand the true-to-life incident of the parable in its full cultural setting, you are better prepared to understand the message of the parable" (Zuck 1991, 211).

What is a Parable?
Examples "A fishing net, a vineyard, a wedding banquet, oil lamps, talents of money, a fig tree still barren after three years, the value of a single coin to a housewife, the people's despicable attitude toward tax collectors, the meaning of pounds or minas – understanding these elements sheds light on the significance of the parables and helps make the right transition to the spiritual truth" (Zuck 1991, 211).

B. Determine the specific problem, occasion, question, need or situation that prompted the parable. Seeing why Jesus told certain parables, when He did, helps us understand the truth He is making in the parable.
- Answering a question, for example, in Matthew 9:14, the disciples of John ask, 'Why do we and the Pharisees fast often, but your disciples fast not?' So Christ gives the parables of the wineskins and the garment to show that His ministry is one of joy (when He is present), and He is not reforming Judaism but replacing it with a new phase of His program.
- Answering a request "The Parable of the Rich Fool (Luke 12:16-21) followed the request made by someone in the crowd that Jesus tell the man's brother to divide their father's inheritance with him (v. 13). Jesus declined to be an arbitrator in that situation and, urging people to be on guard

against greed (vv. 14-15). He then told the Parable of the Rich Fool" (Zuck 1991, 212).

- Answering a complaint When Jesus was criticized for associating with a sinful woman, He gave the Parable of the Two Debtors (Luke 7:40-43).
- Stating a purpose Jesus told the Parable of the Unjust Judge to show His disciples 'that they should always pray and not give up' (Luke 18:1).
- Parables of the Kingdom because of Israel's rejection of Jesus Seven kingdom parables are given in Matthew 13. These parables are significant in that they follow Matthew 12, which records the rejection of Jesus by the Pharisees and the accusation that He was doing His miracles in the power of Satan. The parables of Matthew 13 describe the conditions that will take place between Christ's first coming, His second coming and the establishment of the Kingdom.
- Parables following an exhortation or principle "Several times Jesus gave an exhortation or principle and then followed it with a parable to illustrate or illumine the point just made. For example, Mark 13:33 records that Jesus said, 'Be on guard! Be alert! You do not know when the time will come.' Then He gave the Parable of the Door keeper (vv. 34-37)" (Zuck 1991, 213).
- Parables followed by an exhortation or principle "Sometimes Jesus gave a parable and then followed it with an exhortation or principle. For example, the Parable of the Friend at Midnight (Luke 11:5-8) is followed by His exhortation for them to persist in prayer (vv. 9-10)" (Zuck 1991, 213).
- Parables to illustrate a situation "Jesus introduced the Parable of the Two Houses by pointing up that anyone who heard His words and put them into practice was like the man building a house on a rock (Matt. 7:24)" (Zuck 1991, 214).

- Parables with the purpose implied but not stated "The Parable of the Seed Growing Secretly (Mark 4:26-29) is not stated, but it seems to suggest rapid numerical growth of believers during the present age" (Zuck 1991, 215).

C. Determine the one main point or central truth the parable is attempting to teach "This might be called the golden rule of parabolic interpretation." (Ramm 1970, 283).
   1. Ex. Parable of the Sower (Matt. 13:3-9; 18-23) The main point of this parable is during the present age there will be four different responses to the Gospel.
   2. Ex. Parable of the Dragnet (Matt. 13:47-50) The main point here is that when Christ comes to set up His kingdom, the wicked will be gathered and judged.

D. Do not make a parable walk on all fours "In every parable, many circumstances and details are introduced which are intended merely to complete the similitudes in the parable. The interpreter should not attempt to interpret all such details. A parable ... has but one central truth. Therefore, discover the central truth or theme which the parable is setting forth, and then explain the main circumstances of the parable in light of this truth, leaving out details incidental to its central idea" (Tan 1978, 148). "To hunt for meanings in every detail in the parables is to turn them into allegories" (Zuck 1991, 216).

   1. Ex. The Good Samaritan In the Parable of the Good Samaritan (Luke 10:30-37) the main point is that a neighbor is one who actively helps someone in need. But according to Origen: "The man who fell among thieves is Adam. The robbers are the Devil and his minions. The priest stands for the Law; the Levite for the prophets. The Good Samaritan is Christ; the beast, Christ's body; the inn, the Church; the two pence, the Father and the Son; and the Samaritan's 'When I come again,' Christ's second coming" (Tan 1978, 149). This

117

is reading too much into the parable. As Zuck says, "Jesus did not give any interpretation of the robbers, the man's clothes, the man's wounds, the oil and wine, the donkey, the two silver coins, or the innkeeper. These were elements needed to complete the story and to put it in its proper cultural setting" (Zuck 1991, 216).

2. Ex. Wheat and the Tares "When Christ interprets the Parable of the Tares (Matt. 13:36-43), He explains only the field, the good seed, the tares, the enemy, the harvest, the reapers, and the final events of the harvest. He attaches no significance to the men who slept, the wheat's yielding fruit, the servants, and the question of the servants" (Tan 1978, 149).

3. How do we know what is relevant and incidental in the parable? "Unhappily, there is no determinative key as to what represents relevance in a parable and what is incidental. 'No special rule can be formed that will apply to every case, and show what parts of a parable are designed to be significant, and what parts are mere drapery and form. Sound sense and delicate discrimination are to be cultivated and matured by a protracted study of all the parables, and by careful collation and comparison'" (Tan 1978, 149).

E. Determine how much of the parable is interpreted by the Lord Himself "After reciting the parable of the Sower (Mat. 13:18 ff.) Our Lord interprets it. After stating the parable of the enemy's sowing darnel among the wheat, our Lord interprets it later in the house. In such instances we have the definite word of Christ concerning the meaning of the parable, which further conveys to us the spirit of his teaching for help in parables that are not interpreted" (Ramm 1970, 283).

F. Interpret by proper time periods "There are three main time periods in parabolic prophecies: (1) the inter-advent age, (2) the second coming of Christ, and (3) the millennial age.

The prophetic parables are geared to these different time periods. The interpreter should not try to fit them arbitrarily into one general period, such as the present church age" (Tan 1978, 149).

G. Be careful with doctrine "Parables do teach doctrine, and the claim that they may not be used at all in doctrinal writing is improper. But in gleaning our doctrine from the parables we must be strict in our interpretation; we must check our results with the plain, evident teaching of our Lord, and with the rest of the New Testament. Parables with proper cautions may be used to illustrate doctrine, illumine Christian experience, and to teach practical lessons." (Ramm 1970, 285) For example, the parable of the Ten Virgins does not prove that a person can lose their salvation.

BIBLIOGRAPHY

Alden, Robert L. *Psalms: Volume 3 Songs of Discipleship*, Chicago: Moody Press, 1976.

Allen, Leslie C. *Word Biblical Commentary: Volume 21, Psalms 101-150*, Waco: Word Books Publishers, 1983.

Anthony, Michael J. ed. *Introducing Christian Education: Foundations for the Twenty-first Century*. Grand Rapids: Baker Academic, 2005.

Berkhof, Louis. *Principles of Biblical Interpretation (Sacred Hermeneutics)*. Grand Rapids: Baker Book House, 1984.

Biblesoft's *New Exhaustive Strong's Numbers and Concordance with Expanded Greek-Hebrew Dictionary*. Biblesoft and International Bible Translators, Inc., 1994.

Coleman, William L. *Today's Handbook of Bible Times and Customs*. Chicago: Moody, 1987.

Dillard, Raymond B. and Tremper Longman III. *An Introduction to the Old Testament*. Grand Rapids: Zondervan, 1994.

Elliott E. Johnson, *Expository Hermeneutics: An Introduction*. Grand Rapids: Zondervan Publishing House, 1990.

Ellis, E. Earle. "Pauline Exegesis," in *Paul's Use of the Old Testament*. Eugene, OR: Wipf and Stock Publishers, 2003.

Gibbs, Carl B. *Principles of Biblical Interpretation: An Independent-Study Textbook*, 3rd Ed. Springfield, MO: Global University, 2004.

Gordon, T. David, 1985, http://www.bible-researcher.com/Gordon.html. Accessed on 13 September 2012).

Hartill, J. Edwin. *Principles of Biblical Hermeneutics*, Grand Rapids, MI: Zondervan Publishing House, 1973.

Hendricks, Howard G. and William D. Hendricks. Living by the Book. Chicago: Moody Press, 1991.

Interlinear Transliterated Bible. Biblesoft, 1994.

Kaiser, Walter C. Jr. *A History of Israel.* Nashville, TN: Broadman and Holman, 1998.

Kaiser, Walter C. Jr. *Toward an Exegetical Theology: Biblical Exegesis for Preaching and Teaching.* Grand Rapids: Baker Book House, 1994.

Keck, Leander E., ed. *The New Interpreter's Bible: Volume IV,* Nashville, TN: Abingdon Press, 1976.

Klein, William W., Craig L. Blomberg, and Robert L. Hubbard, Jr. *Introduction to Biblical Interpretation.* Dallas, TX: Word Publishing, 1994.

Leslie, Elmer A. *The Psalms:* Nashville, TN: Abingdon Press, 1949.

Lewis, Stephen R., *Bible 405: Hermeneutics: The Study of the Interpretation of Scriptures. Accessed at http://www.church ofhopeontheweb.org/Hermeneutics.pdf* (Chafer Theological Seminary) on December 2006.

Lowenberg, Douglas P. *Current Issues in New Testament Interpretation: Doctoral Study Guide.* Lome: Pan-Africa Theological Seminary, 2005.

Lowenberg, Douglas P. *Current Issues in Old Testament Interpretation: Doctoral Study Guide.* Lome: Pan-Africa Theological Seminary, 2006.

McEachern, Alton H. *Layman's Bible Book Commentary: Psalms Volume 8.* Nashville, TN: Broadman Press, 1981.

Packer, J. I., Merrill C. Tenney and William White, Jr. *The Bible Almanac.* Nashville: Thomas Nelson, 1980.

Parker, T.H.L. *Calvin's New Testament Commentaries*. Grand Rapids: Eerdmans, 1971.

Ramm, Bernard, *Protestant Biblical Interpretation*. Grand Rapids: MI: Baker Book House, 1970.

Ramm, Bernard. *Protestant Biblical Interpretation*, 3rd ed. Grand Rapids, MI: Baker Book House, 1995.

Robertson's Word Pictures in the New Testament, Electronic Database. 1997 by Biblesoft and Robertson's Word Pictures in the New Testament. Nashville, TN: Broadman Press, 1985.

Samworth, Herbert. (http://www.solagroup.org/articles/historyof thebible/hotb_0003.html).

Sandy, D. Brent and Ronald L. Griese, Jr. *Cracking Old Testament Codes*. Nashville, TN: Broadman and Holman, 1995.

Smith, Gary V. *The Prophets as Preachers*. Nashville, TN: Broadman and Holman, 1994.

Stamps, Donald C., ed. *The Full Life Study Bible: New International Version*. Grand Rapids, MI: Zondervan Publishing House, 1992.

Summers, Della. *Longman Dictionary Contemporary English*, 3rd ed. Edinburgh Gate: Pearson Education Limited, 2001.

Tan, Paul Lee. The Interpretation of Prophecy. Rockwille: Assurance Press, 1978.

Terry, Milton S. *Biblical Hermeneutics: A Treatise on the Interpretation of the Old and New Testaments*. Grand Rapids, MI: Zondervan Publishing House, 1978.

Vincent's Word Studies of the New Testament, Electronic Database. Biblesoft, 1997.

Virkler, Henry A., *Hermeneutics: Principles and Processes of Biblical Interpretation*. Grand Rapids: Baker, 1981.

Vlach, Mike, *Hermeneutics: Principles of Bible Interpretation*: Part 2 of 2 Indian Hills Community Church Center for Biblical Studies, Lincoln, www.ihcc.org. (http://storage.cloversites.com/journey thruthebiblesundayschoolclass/documents/Biblical%20Hermeneu tics_2.pdf. Accessed on 12th April 2015)

Walvoord, John F., *The Millennial Kingdom*. Grand Rapids: Zondervan, 1959.

Wenham, John W. "Jesus' View of the Old Testament," in *Christ and the Bible*.

Zuck, Roy B. Basic Bible Interpretation: A Practical Guide to Discovering Biblical Truth. Glasgow: Victor Books, 1991.

Zuck, Roy B. (ed). Rightly Divided: Readings in Biblical Hermeneutics. Grand Rapids: Kregel Publishers, 1996.

Printed in the United States
By Bookmasters